*P. 5° Pray
St. michael Prayer every day !*

Devotion to the Most Precious Blood of Our Lord Jesus Christ

The Greatest Devotion of our time
A Call to Holiness

Queenship

PUBLISHING COMPANY
P.O. Box 220 • Goleta, CA 93116
(800) 647-9882 • (805) 692-0043 • Fax: (805) 967-5133

©2005 Queenship Publishing — All rights reserved.

ISBN: 1-57918-272-0

Published by:
  Queenship Publishing
  P.O. Box 220
  Goleta, CA 93116
  (800) 647-9882 • (805) 692-0043 • Fax: (805) 967-5133
  www.queenship.org

Printed in the United States of America

TABLE OF CONTENTS

NIHIL OBSTAT:
>Rev. Fr. Stephen Obiukwu
>Censor Deputatus
>Chairman, Doctrine and Faith Committee
>Archdiocese of Onitsha, Anambra State
>NIGERIA
>1st July, 1999.

IMPRIMATUR:
>Ayo-Maria Atoyebi, O.P.
>Bishop of Ilorin Diocese
>Ilorin, Kwara State NIGERIA
>17th June, 2001.

HEAD OFFICE:
>Apostolate of the Precious Blood of Jesus Christ
>Land of Adoration, Rock of Gethsemane
>Olo, Ezeagu L.G.A., Enugu, Enugu State 400001
>NIGERIA
>Telephone:(Int'l access code +) 234 - 803 – 345-0253
>   (Int'l access code +) 234 - 803 – 379-2866
>Email: precious_blood2000@yahoo.com

HEAD OFFICE POSTAL ADDRESS:
>Apostolate of the Precious Blood of Jesus Christ
>P O Box 121 – Iwollo
>Enugu, Enugu State 401006 NIGERIA

BISHOP'S ADDRESS:
>Bishop's House, Communications Centre
>P.O. Box 686
>Ilorin, Kwara State 240001 NIGERIA

Dedication

This book is dedicated to
the Agonizing and Sorrowful Hearts
of Jesus and Mary
Who still suffer mystically
the pains caused by this sinful world.
May our little gesture of love ~
for these Two Loving Hearts
in this Devotion ~
appease their pain.
Amen.

From left a nun of the Apostolate, Barnabas' brother Benjamin, the visionary Barnabas, Bishop Ayo Maria of Ilorin who the Lord Himself named the spiritual Director and Patron of the Apostolate, Barnabas' Spiritual Director, Rev. Fr. Boniface Onah, Barnabas' brother Josephat and his sister Irene who told Barnabas to start recording Heaven's revelations.

CHRIST'S BLOOD, SOURCE OF SALVATION

OUR HOLY FATHER, POPE JOHN PAUL II, ADDRESSES RELIGIOUS FAMILIES AND CATHOLIC ASSOCIATIONS DEVOTED TO THE PRECIOUS BLOOD.

Dear Brothers and Sisters!

1. I am pleased to meet you all, members of the male and female religious families and Catholic associations devoted to the Most Precious Blood of Jesus on this first day of July, which Christian piety has dedicated to meditation on "the Blood of Christ, the price of our redemption, the pledge of salvation and eternal life." *(John XXIII, Apostolic Letter "Inde a primis" in AAS, 52 (1960 545-550).* As I greet you affectionately and thank you for coming, I extend my gratitude to the Provincial Director of the Society of the Precious Blood for his kind words, which he also addressed to me in your name.

Until the liturgical reform introduced by the Second Vatican Council, on this day (July 1ˢᵗ), the mystery of the Blood of Christ was also liturgically celebrated throughout the Catholic Church. Paul VI, my predecessor of venerable memory, joined the commemoration of the Blood of Christ with that of His Body in what is now called the Solemnity of the "Body and Blood of Christ." For in every Eucharistic celebration, not only does the Body of Christ become present, but also His Precious Blood, the Blood of the new and everlasting covenant which is shed for all so that sins may be forgiven. (cf. Mt. 26:27).

2. Dear brothers and sisters, what a great mystery is the Blood of Christ! From the dawn of Christianity it has captivated the minds and hearts of so many Christians and particularly of your holy founders and foundresses, who made it the standard of your congregations and associations. The Jubilee Year gives new impetus to this impor-

tant devotion. For, as we celebrate Christ 2000 years after His birth, we are also invited to contemplate and adore Him in His Sacred Humanity, assumed in Mary's womb and hypostatically united to the Divine Person of the Word. Christ's Blood is the precious source of salvation for the world precisely because it belongs to the Word who became flesh for our salvation.

The sign of "blood poured out," as an expression of life given in bloodshed as a witness to supreme love, is an act of divine condescension to our human condition. God chose the sign of blood because no other sign suggests a person's total involvement so eloquently.

This mystery of self-giving has its source in the Heavenly Father's salvific Will and it's fulfillment in the filial obedience of Jesus, true God and true Man, through the work of the Holy Spirit. Thus the history of our salvation bears the mark and indelible seal of Trinitarian love.

3. In the presence of this wondrous divine work, all the faithful join you, dear brothers and sisters, in offering hymns of praise to the Triune God in the sign of Christ's Precious Blood. However, the witness of life must be joined with the confession of the lips, as we are urged by the Letter to the Hebrews: "Therefore, brethren, since we have confidence to enter the sanctuary by the Blood of Jesus…let us consider how to stir up one another to love and good works." (Heb 10:19, 24)

And there are many "good works" which meditation on Christ's sacrifice inspires in us. It spurs us, in fact, to give our life for God and our brethren without reserve, "usque ad effusionem sanguinis," as so many martyrs have done. How could we ever fail to recognize the value of every human being, when Christ shed his Blood for each one without distinction? Meditation on this mystery prompts us to turn to all those whose moral and physical suffering could be alleviated but who, instead, are left to languish on the fringes of an affluent and indifferent society. It is in this perspective that your service…stands out in all its nobility. You do not limit yourselves to giving something that belongs to you; you give something of yourselves. What is more personal than one's own blood? In the light of Christ, the gift of this vital element to a brother or sister acquires a value that transcends mere human horizons.

Dear friends, may the celebration of the 2,000[th] anniversary of the Incarnation of the Son of God find you watchful in faith, firm in hope and fervent in charity. Today Christ still approaches each person to offer him the gift of God's infinite mercy. May you also be rich in this mercy, as is our Father in heaven.

With these sentiments and in the love of the One who has sprinkled us with his blood (cf. 1 Pt 1:2), I wholeheartedly bless you all.

(Address of 1 July 2000, as he welcomed members of the various religious families and Catholic associations devoted to the Precious Blood, volunteers of the Italian Blood Donor's Association and different Italian pilgrim groups)

DEVOTION TO
THE MOST PRECIOUS BLOOD
OF OUR LORD JESUS CHRIST

Glory be to Jesus and Mary!
Unto life everlasting!

Devotion to the Most Precious Blood of Our Lord Jesus Christ is not a new one in the Holy Catholic Church. It is as old as the first Holy Thursday when Jesus Christ instituted the Priesthood and the Holy Eucharist. The proclamation of the following words on the night before He suffered, "This is My Body, which is given for you. Do this in memory of Me...This cup is God's new covenant sealed with My Blood which is poured for you," (Lk. 22:19-20) evoked from the Apostles a sublime religious fervor or reverence. Before then Jesus had performed great miracles but they saw the miracle of miracles in the institution of the Holy Eucharist, the Sacrifice of the Cross, the Sacrifice of the New Law, the most admirable Sacrament, the wondrous presence, and the abiding memorial of Christ's Passion. Seeing Christ setting Himself before them as a sacrifice of reconciliation or salvation and as the food of eternal life in the most precious and wonderful banquet, made them adore the wondrous presence with a faith beyond description. Since then it has always been so in the Holy Catholic Church and it will continue to be so until the Lord comes back in glory. That is the Lord's command. We must continue to proclaim the Lord's death until He returns. (cf. I Cor. 11:26).

As long as the Church continues to celebrate the Holy Eucharist in obedience to the Lord's command, "Do this in memory of Me," she maintains throughout time her devotion to the Precious Blood and Body of Our Lord Jesus Christ. She offers a living sacrifice, a perpetual memorial of His Passion which demonstrates the immensity of Christ's love for us. The best way for each one of us to show our devotion to the Eucharistic Lord is to receive Him in Holy Communion and participate actively and reverently in Holy Mass. If we know truly that the Eucharist is the Sacrifice of the Cross we will worship more with greater attention and devotion and resist all tendencies to turn the Mass into a disco room or a fund-raising gathering.

The Mass is the re-enactment of the paschal mystery. It is at the same time the sacrificial memorial in which the Sacrifice of the Cross is perpetuated and also the sacred banquet of communion with the Lord's Body and Blood. In the Mass we become one with Jesus and with one another. Our souls are filled with grace and a pledge of future glory is given to us. All these inestimable treasures deserve our devotion. Devotion to the Eucharistic Lord continues in the Benediction, frequent visitation to the Lord in the Blessed Sacrament and exposition of the Blessed Sacrament. In this we also see the devotion to the Precious Blood of Jesus because as a living person His Blood cannot be separated from His Body.

The Chaplet of the Most Precious Blood

In the Devotion to Divine Mercy, our worship is centered on the Precious Blood of Jesus. The Precious Blood is the "source of life which gushed forth for souls." We pray, "O Blood and Water which gushed forth from the Heart of Jesus as a fount of mercy for us, I trust in You." We continually offer the Body and Blood of Jesus to the Eternal Father in atonement for our sins and the sins of the whole world. It is interesting to note the similarity between the response said on the ten beads of the Chaplet of Divine Mercy and that of the twelve beads of the Chaplet of the Precious Blood.

On the ten beads of Divine Mercy Chaplet we respond *"have mercy on us and on the whole world"* while on the twelve beads of the Precious Blood Chaplet we say *"save us and the whole world."* This depicts a common concern coming from the same divine source. No true devotion contradicts another but one complements the other.

Furthermore, these devotions are Eucharistic devotions. They recall in contemplation the events we celebrate in the Eucharist. They can be used as preparation or thanksgiving for Holy Mass. Some are opposed to a variety of devotions; they ask "why are you dividing

Christ?" Some devote themselves to the Sacred Heart, the Holy Face, the Holy Wounds, the Precious Blood, etc. Christ is manifold. He is infinite! No one can exhaust Him in one devotion or another. One compliments the other and all meet in Christ. Jesus is not against this. He reveals one aspect of the mystery of salvation at a time most appropriate to Him to draw us to Him. Instead of quarrelling about too many devotions we should thank God for the inestimable riches in these Catholic devotions.

Contemplate Christ with Mary

In Mama Maria's Holy Rosary given to St. Dominic, God gives us the compendium of the New Testament of the life, death and resurrection of Jesus and our own future glory to meditate upon. We pray along with Mama Maria in the Rosary. We should continue to do this. No child of Mary should sleep without having prayed the Rosary with Mary as he or she joins all Marian children in the world. It is rewarding and very powerful to pray the Rosary and live her life. It is a sign of predestination to Heaven to have devotion to Mary.

Eucharistic devotion, Divine Mercy devotion, renewal of devotion to Mary and the Chaplet of the Precious Blood are rare gifts of the present critical time which may become turbulent if we do not use these gifts. The Chaplet of the Precious Blood with devotion to the Wounds of the Lord Jesus is a spiritual gift of inestimable price for this critical time. We focus all our attention on the Crucified Lord. What makes this Chaplet very powerful is that we stand before the Cross of Jesus with Our Blessed Mother, Our Lady of Sorrows, the Co-Redemptrix, Our Advocate and Mediatrix of all graces. Our gazes are on the Five Wounds of Jesus and the Blood and Water He shed from them.

We plead His Wounds and Blood with Our Blessed Mother because the days are evil. (Eph. 5:16). We need to fly to the patronage of the Most Blessed Virgin, through total dedication and consecration to her Immaculate Heart, the Sacred Heart of Jesus, and the Most Precious Blood as our protective armors in order to be able to stand up against all diabolical tricks and attacks. (cf. Eph. 6:10-13). The mysteries are about mystical things; they pertain to the ultimate things of the kingdom, the glory of God, the salvation of souls and the well-being of the faithful. The Chaplet is a very powerful prayer. Like all powerful things of the realm of the spirit, it is simple, elevating and full of consolation. It covers both universal and individual needs. It is a powerful means of defense, salvation, deliverance and fortification. Anyone who faithfully devotes himself or herself to the Divine Blood of Jesus cannot but be heard and endowed with the choicest gifts by Him Who has all power in Heaven and on Earth. (cf. Mt. 28:18).

The antics and evil machinations of Satan cannot but be destroyed in your life when you live a good life and confront him and his agents with the same Precious Blood that threw him down from his usurped throne.

Other Values of the Devotion

The Chaplet of the Most Precious Blood is a means of glorifying God for the immensity of His love shown to us by giving up His only-begotten Son on the Cross. (Jn. 3:16). It is an unfailing means of tapping the inexhaustible mercy of God from the source of our salvation. No one who is devoted to the Wounds and Blood of Jesus can be lost. The darts of the evil one cannot touch them as the angel of death did not visit the houses of the Israelites marked with the blood of the lambs. (cf. Ex. 12:1-36). So also the Lord assures the safety, security and freedom of those who honor His Wounds and Blood. Gazing on the Lord on the Cross challenges us to be virtuous like Him, to live for God's glory, to eradicate selfishness in our lives and to hold to the truth of God and His commands even if we have to die.

Through this Chaplet of the Precious Blood, we apply the merits of Jesus' Blood and Wounds for healing and for deliverance because, "it is by His Wounds that we can be healed." (cf. I Pt. 2:24). We can ask for personal needs and particular concerns for ourselves and others, using the Chaplet of the Most Precious Blood in different forms of novenas. Families or individuals that have no peace will soon glorify the Lord when He gives them the peace that the world cannot give (cf. Jn. 14:27) as they pray this Chaplet. Recommend the Chap-

let of the Precious Blood to others. Join those devoted to the Holy
Wounds and the Precious Blood of Jesus in their devotion. Only the
spiritually blind people will deny that the time is bad. Make it good
for yourself and others by praying the Chaplet of the Most Precious
Blood and cover yourself and the whole world in the Most Precious
Blood of Our Lord Jesus Christ. A trial will definitely convince you.
May the Precious Blood of Mercy save us and the whole world as
Our Lady pleads for us. Through Christ Our Lord. Amen.

Ayo-Maria Atoyebi, OP
Bishop of Ilorin Diocese (Nigeria)
June 17, 2001
Solemnity of the Body and Blood of Christ.

A SUMMARY OF
THE PRECIOUS BLOOD DEVOTION

In 1995, at exactly 3:00pm, the hour of Divine Mercy, Our Lord Jesus Christ called for the first time Barnabas Nwoye, a teenager from Olo, Enugu State, Nigeria, and appealed to him to console Him and to adore His Precious Blood. In a vision two years later, the Lord gave him the Chaplet of the Precious Blood and all its component prayers. The messages, prayers, hymns and choruses, as well as the instructions given directly by Our Lord, His Mother Mary, the Angels and Saints, between 1997 and 2003, constitute the Precious Blood Devotion in this publication.Summed up, the Devotion is made up of the following:

1. Chaplet
The Chaplet of the Precious Blood, to be recited immediately after saying the Rosary of the Blessed Virgin Mary, consists of Five Mysteries relating to the Five Sacred Wounds of Christ.

2. Consolation
Consolation Prayers directed to the Eternal Father and His only-begotten Son constitute the second segment of this Devotion. These prayers seek to appease the Father and the Son for the world's ingratitude, blasphemies and neglects of the Precious Blood.

3. Adoration
In the third part of the Devotion, one finds seven prayers which adore, glorify and make petitions to the Precious Blood. The petitions are for the entire Church, its hierarchy, the clergy and the faithful.

Appeals invoking the Precious Blood are also made on behalf of unrepentant sinners, souls in purgatory, non-Catholics, for devout souls and for aborted babies that they may all be accorded the benefits of the Precious Blood.

4. Reparation

The fourth segment of the Devotion deals with reparation. In the seven Anguished Appeals, Our Lord describes the various sins in the Church and in the world at large that have mystically continued to crucify Him. These include neglect of the Holy Sacrifice of the Mass and the Sacraments by the clergy and the faithful, immodesty which is causing millions to march into Hell, materialism in the Church and the world, cultism, greed, avarice and so on.

5. Intercession

Besides the four principal parts, there are key intercessory prayers which Our Lord has revealed as the prayers He said during His Passion and before His final human breath for our salvation. They include prayers to defeat all enemies of the Holy Cross (the Anti-Christ and his forces), for faith, endurance, for release from ancestral curses and so on.

6. The Seal

One will discover from this Devotion about the Great Seal of God, the living Tabernacle in our Hearts, without which one will carry the enemy's own seal of 666. The Great Seal is obtained by perpetually struggling to remain in a state of Sanctifying Grace, especially within the specified periods when the Angels tour the earth to place the Seal.

7. Gethsemane Hour

Finally, through this Devotion Our Lord is calling on His chosen people to observe every Thursday night into Friday morning from 11:00pm to 3:00am, as the Gethsemane Hour of Prayer during which the first four components of this Devotion should be observed, or at least one hour between 12:00am and 3:00am. The intention is to obtain grace to endure the Great Chastisement.

Call to Holiness

The Precious Blood Devotion is a daily call to holiness. At least one of the Mysteries of the Rosary of Our Blessed Mother, followed by the Chaplet, the Precious Blood Litany, and the Consecration must be recited daily by a devotee. This Devotion is the ultimate weapon against Satan and evil spirits.

Above all, the Devotion is a way of life. The Lord describes it as "the dry and desert way" full of crosses. It is a reminder that only through the cross can a soul reach the land of happiness, which is Heaven. Any other way will result in Hell. It is a holy call to Catholics and all Christians to return to the True Faith in a corrupt world, deceived by Satan, in which all sorts of Gospels are now being preached even within Catholicism.

Through this Devotion, Our Lord has announced the birth of the Triumph of the Immaculate Heart of Mary and His Glorious Reign on earth. The world should, henceforth, mark September 14th as the feast day of the Triumph of the Two Hearts of Love. So has the Lord directed. What remains to unravel in the days ahead is the final showdown between good and evil that will usher in this New Era.

Every prayer, every hymn and every chorus of this Devotion came straight from Heaven.

THE HOLY ROSARY
OF THE BLESSED VIRGIN MARY

"My son, pray your Holy Rosary always as My Mother has ordered you. Pray the Holy Chaplet of My Precious Blood immediately after your Holy Rosary. You must do this because the hour of salvation is very short." (19 January 1997)

OPENING PRAYERS

*Note, prayers printed with asterick are found on
page 95 - 97 in the prayer appendix.

Sign of the Cross*
…State your intentions for this Rosary…

*Suggested Offering: I unite with all the Angels and Saints in heaven,
the poor souls in purgatory, all the Masses and prayers that have
ever been, or ever will be prayed; all the tears, joys, sacrifices and
sufferings of every soul who ever has, or ever will live. I unite it all to
the Sorrowful Heart of Mary at the foot of the Cross and offer Jesus
the whole of creation with it; for the conversion of sinners, the relief
of the souls in Purgatory, the sanctification of priests and religious,
the desires of The Two Hearts, peace in the world, and for my intentions (mention them here).*

Apostle's Creed*…Our Father*
…Hail Mary* (3 times)…Glory Be*..

THE JOYFUL MYSTERIES

1. **The Annunciation**
L: May the Lord Jesus Christ grant us all pro found humility.
R: Amen.

Hymn
(music on page 97)
Jesus in the Holy Eucharist
We are sorry
For all the sins
Committed against You on earth.

Invocation
L: St. Michael the Archangel, with your light,
R: Enlighten us.
L: With your wings,

R: Protect us.
L: With your sword,
R: Defend us.

Prayers
Our Father*...Hail Mary* (10 times)...
Glory Be*...O my Jesus*...

2. **The Visitation**
   L: May the Lord grant us perfect charity towards our neighbor.
   R: Amen.

   Repeat Hymn, Invocation, and Prayers

3. **The Nativity**
   L: May the Lord grant us the grace of love of poverty and love
   of the poor.
   R: Amen.

   Repeat Hymn, Invocation, and Prayers

4. **The Presentation of Jesus in the Temple**
   L: May the Lord grant us the gift of wisdom and purity of heart,
   mind and body.
   R: Amen.

   Repeat Hymn, Invocation, and Prayers

5. **The Finding of Jesus in the Temple**
   L: May the Lord further convert us and convert all sinners in
   the world.
   R: Amen.

   Repeat Hymn, Invocation, and Prayers

THE LUMINOUS MYSTERIES

1. **The Baptism of Our Lord**
   L: May the Lord grant us the grace to live our baptismal vows,
   the life of our consecration.
   R: Amen.

Hymn

(music on page 97)
Let us sing with you Virgin Mother
And love with you
Your Son, Our Lord
Jesus Christ Who died for us

Invocation

(see page 2)

Prayers

Our Father*...Hail Mary* (10 times)...
Glory Be*...O my Jesus*...

2. **Jesus Manifests Himself at Cana**
   L: May the Lord grant healing to ailing marriages and increase
   our faith in Mary's intercession.
   R: Amen.

   Repeat Hymn, Invocation, and Prayers

3. **Jesus Proclaims the Kingdom of God**
   L: May the Lord grant us the holiness required to become true
   sons and daughters of God's Kingdom on earth.
   R: Amen.

   Repeat Hymn, Invocation, and Prayers

4. **The Transfiguration of Our Lord**
   L: May the Precious Blood of Christ sanctify and transform us
   all into a holy nation.
   R: Amen.

   Repeat Hymn, Invocation, and Prayers

5. **The Institution of the Holy Eucharist**
   L: May the Lord grant us the grace to cherish the Most Holy
   Eucharist by receiving it worthily and by loving our
   ordained priests and praying for them.
   R: Amen.

   Repeat Hymn, Invocation, and Prayers

THE SORROWFUL MYSTERIES

1. **The Agony in the Garden of Gethsemane**
   L: May the Lord grant us perfect sorrow for our sins and the
   virtue of perfect obedience to His will.
   R: Amen.

Hymn
(music on page 97)
For Your Precious Blood shed for mankind,
We are sorry,
For all the sins,
Committed against You O Lord.

Invocation
(see page 2)

Prayers
Our Father*...Hail Mary* (10 times)...
Glory Be*...O My Jesus*...

2. **Scourging of Jesus at the Pillar**
   L: May the Lord grant us the grace of mortifying our senses
   perfectly.
   R: Amen.

Repeat Hymn, Invocation, and Prayers

3. **Our Lord is Crowned with Thorns**
   L: May the Lord grant us the grace of a great contempt for the
   world.
   R: Amen.

Repeat Hymn, Invocation, and Prayers

4. **Our Lord Carries His Cross**
   L: May the Lord grant us the grace of patiently carrying our
   own crosses everyday of our lives in imitation of his
   footsteps.
   R: Amen.

Repeat Hymn, Invocation, and Prayers

5. **Crucifixion and Death of Our Lord**
    L: May the Lord grant us the grace of horror of sin, love of the
       Cross and holy death for ourselves. May He also be
       merciful to all those in their last agony.
    R: Amen

    Repeat Hymn, Invocation, and Prayers

THE GLORIOUS MYSTERIES

1. **The Resurrection**
    L: May the Lord grant us the grace of a lively faith.
    R: Amen

    Hymn
    (music on page 97)
    Flood the whole human race
    With your flame,
    Your flame of love,
    Oh! Blessed Virgin
    Now and at the hour of our death.

    Invocation
    (see page 2)

    Prayers
    Our Father*...Hail Mary* (10 times)...
    Glory Be*...O My Jesus*...

2. **The Ascension of Jesus Christ into Heaven**
    L: May the Lord grant us all firm hope and a great longing for
       Heaven.
    R: Amen.

    Repeat Hymn, Invocation, and Prayers

3. **The Descent of the Holy Spirit**
    L: May the Lord grant us divine wisdom to know, love and
       practice divine truth and to make others share in it.

R: Amen.

Repeat Hymn, Invocation, and Prayers

4. **The Assumption of Our Blessed Mother Mary into Heaven**
    L: May the Lord grant us the precious gift and privilege of true
       devotion to Our Mother Mary to help us live and die as the
       Saints before us.
    R: Amen.

Repeat Hymn, Invocation, and Prayers

5. **The Crowning of the Blessed Virgin Mary as Queen of
    Heaven and Earth**
    L: May the Lord grant the grace to Christians who do not know
       Mary and who do not love and honor her to appreciate her
       maternal assistance and virtues as the shortest, most whole
       some and easiest way to Christ's heart.
    R: Amen

Repeat Hymn, Invocation, and Prayers

Hail Holy Queen*… Sign of the Cross*…

LITANY OF THE
BLESSED VIRGIN MARY

Lord, have mercy	Lord, have mercy
Christ, have mercy	Christ, have mercy
Lord, have mercy	Lord, have mercy
Christ, hear us	Christ, graciously hear us
God, the Father of Heaven	have mercy on us
God the Son, Redeemer of the World	have mercy on us
God, the Holy Spirit	have mercy on us
Holy Trinity, One God	have mercy on us
Holy Mary	pray for us
Holy Mother of God	pray for us
Holy Virgin of Virgins	pray for us
Mother of Christ	pray for us
Mother of Divine Grace	pray for us

Mother of the Church	pray for us
Mother most Pure	pray for us
Mother most chaste	pray for us
Mother inviolate	pray for us
Mother undefiled	pray for us
Mother most amiable	pray for us
Mother most admirable	pray for us
Mother of Good Counsel	pray for us
Mother of Our Creator	pray for us
Mother of Our Savior	pray for us
Virgin most prudent	pray for us
Virgin most venerable	pray for us
Virgin most renowned	pray for us
Virgin most powerful	pray for us
Virgin most merciful	pray for us
Virgin most faithful	pray for us
Mirror of justice	pray for us
Seat of wisdom	pray for us
Cause of our joy	pray for us
Spiritual vessel	pray for us
Vessel of honor	pray for us
Singular vessel of devotion	pray for us
Mystical Rose	pray for us
Tower of David	pray for us
Tower of ivory	pray for us
House of gold	pray for us
Ark of the Covenant	pray for us
Gate of Heaven	pray for us
Morning Star	pray for us
Health of the sick	pray for us
Refuge of sinners	pray for us
Comforter of the afflicted	pray for us
Help of Christians	pray for us
Queen of Angels	pray for us
Queen of Patriarchs	pray for us
Queen of Prophets	pray for us
Queen of Apostles	pray for us

Queen of Martyrs	pray for us
Queen of Confessors	pray for us
Queen of Virgins	pray for us
Queen of all Saints	pray for us
Queen conceived without original sin	pray for us
Queen assumed into Heaven	pray for us
Queen of the most Holy Rosary	pray for us
Queen of Peace	pray for us

L: Lamb of God, Who takes away the sins of the world;
R: Spare us, O Lord.
L: Lamb of God, Who takes away the sins of the world;
R: Graciously hear us, O Lord.
L: Lamb of God, Who takes away the sins of the world;
R: Have mercy on us.
L: Pray for us, O Holy Mother of God
R: That we may be made worthy of the promises of Christ.

Let us Pray

Grant, we beseech You O Lord God, that we Your servants may enjoy lasting health of mind and body; and by the glorious intercession of Blessed Mary Ever-Virgin, be delivered from present sorrow and enter into the joy of eternal happiness, through Christ Our Lord. Amen.
L: May the Divine assistance remain always with us.
R: And may the souls of all the faithful departed, through the mercy of God, rest in peace. Amen.

Prayers for the Pope
Our Father*... Hail Mary*... Glory Be*...
A Hymn to the Blessed Virgin...

Note: *The Litany of the Blessed Virgin Mary and a hymn in her honor are recited as a part of the Rosary format of the Apostolate of the Precious Blood. Since Our Lord simply requested that we pray the Rosary immediately followed by the Chaplet, you may use any Rosary devotion in place of this one.*

© 1990 Janet's Illustrations

"My children, this Chaplet of the Precious Blood of my Son combines all devotions of my Son's Passion." (29 January 1997)

CHAPLET OF THE PRECIOUS BLOOD
(15 March 1997)

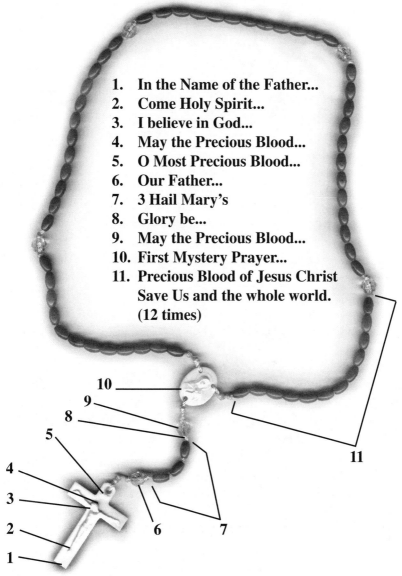

1. In the Name of the Father...
2. Come Holy Spirit...
3. I believe in God...
4. May the Precious Blood...
5. O Most Precious Blood...
6. Our Father...
7. 3 Hail Mary's
8. Glory be...
9. May the Precious Blood...
10. First Mystery Prayer...
11. Precious Blood of Jesus Christ Save Us and the whole world. (12 times)

"My son, take this chaplet, show it to the world. Let everyone pray it always and make constant reparation for all the sins committed against My Precious Blood. Produce this chaplet and make use of it in your prayers. I will use this chaplet to perform great miracles." (15 March 1997)

OPENING PRAYERS

Sign of the Cross*…

Hymn
(Music on page 98)
Most Precious Blood of Jesus Christ
Most Precious Blood of Jesus Christ
Most Precious Blood of Jesus Christ
Most Precious Blood of Jesus Christ
Most Precious Blood, save the world.

Prayer to the Holy Spirit
Come, O Holy Spirit, fill the hearts of Your faithful and enkindle in
them the fire of Your love. Send forth Your Spirit and they shall be
created. And You shall renew the face of the earth.
L: Let us pray.
O God, Who by the light of the Holy Spirit did instruct the hearts of
the faithful, grant that by the same Holy Spirit we may be truly wise
and ever rejoice in His consolation, through Christ Our Lord. Amen.

Apostles Creed*…(On crucifix)

(Bow Your Head)
May the Precious Blood that pours out from the Sacred Head of Our
Lord Jesus Christ, the Temple of Divine Wisdom, the Tabernacle of
Divine Knowledge and the Sunshine of Heaven and earth, cover us
now and forever. Amen.

L: O Most Precious Blood of Jesus Christ.
R: Heal the Wounds in the Most Sacred Heart of Jesus.

Our Father* … Hail Mary* (3 times)… Glory Be* …

(Bow Your Head)
May the Precious Blood that pours out from the Sacred Head of
Our Lord Jesus Christ, the Temple of Divine Wisdom, the Tabernacle of Divine Knowledge and the Sunshine of Heaven and earth,
cover us now and forever. Amen.

THE FIRST MYSTERY
The Nailing of the Right Hand of Our Lord Jesus
(Pause for brief meditation)

By the Precious Wound in Your Right Hand and through the pain of the nail which pierced Your Right Hand, may the Precious Blood that pours out from there, convert many souls and save sinners of the whole world. Amen.

L: O Most Precious Blood of Jesus Christ.
R: Heal the Wounds in the Most Sacred Heart of Jesus.

Our Father*... Hail Mary*...(both on white bead)

L: Precious Blood of Jesus Christ.
R: Save us and the whole world. (12 times)

Glory be to the Father*...

(Bow Your Head)

May the Precious Blood that pours out from the Sacred Head of Our Lord Jesus Christ, the Temple of Divine Wisdom, the Tabernacle of Divine Knowledge and the Sunshine of Heaven and earth cover us now and forever. Amen.

THE SECOND MYSTERY
The Nailing of the Left Hand of Our Lord Jesus
(Pause to meditate)

By the Precious Wound in Your Left Hand and through the pain of the nail which pierced Your Left Hand, may the Precious Blood that pours out from there relieve souls in Purgatory and protect the dying against the attacks of infernal spirits. Amen.

L: O Most Precious Blood of Jesus Christ.
R: Heal the Wounds in the Most Sacred Heart of Jesus

Our Father*... Hail Mary*...

L: Precious Blood of Jesus Christ.
R: Save us and the whole world. (12 times)

Glory be to the Father*...

(Bow Your Head)
May the Precious Blood that pours out from the Sacred Head of Our Lord Jesus Christ, the Temple of Divine Wisdom, the Tabernacle of Divine Knowledge and the Sunshine of Heaven and earth cover us now and forever. Amen.

THE THIRD MYSTERY
The Nailing of the Right Foot of Our Lord Jesus
(Pause to meditate)
By the Precious Wound in Your Right Foot and through the pain of the nail which pierced Your Right Foot, may the Precious Blood that pours out from there cover the foundation of the Catholic Church against the plans of the occult kingdom and evil men. Amen.

L: O Most Precious Blood of Jesus Christ.
R: Heal the Wounds in the Most Sacred Heart of Jesus.

Our Father*... Hail Mary*...

L: Precious Blood of Jesus Christ.
R: Save us and the whole world. (12 times)

Glory be to the Father*...

(Bow Your Head)
May the Precious Blood that pours out from the Sacred Head of Our Lord Jesus Christ, the Temple of Divine Wisdom, the Tabernacle of Divine Knowledge and the Sunshine of Heaven and earth cover us now and forever. Amen.

THE FOURTH MYSTERY
The Nailing of the Left Foot of Our Lord Jesus

(Pause to meditate)

By the Precious Wound in Your Left Foot, and through the pain of the nail which pierced Your Left Foot, may the Precious Blood that pours out from there protect us in all our ways against the plans and the attacks of evil spirits and their agents. Amen.

L: O Most Precious Blood of Jesus Christ.
R: Heal the Wounds in the Most Sacred Heart of Jesus.

Our Father*... Hail Mary*...

L: Precious Blood of Jesus Christ.
R: Save us and the whole world. (12 times)

Glory be to the Father*...

(Bow Your Head)

May the Precious Blood that pours out from the Sacred Head of Our Lord Jesus Christ, the Temple of Divine Wisdom, the Tabernacle of Divine Knowledge and the Sunshine of Heaven and earth cover us now and forever. Amen.

THE FIFTH MYSTERY
The Piercing of the Sacred Side of Our Lord Jesus
(Pause to meditate)

By the Precious Wound in Your Sacred Side and through the pain of the lance which pierced Your Sacred Side, may the Precious Blood and Water that pours out from there cure the sick, raise the dead, solve our present problems and teach us the way to our God for eternal glory. Amen.

L: O Most Precious Blood of Jesus Christ.
R: Heal the Wounds in the most Sacred Heart of Jesus.

Our Father*... Hail Mary*...

L: Precious Blood of Jesus Christ.

R: Save us and the whole world. (12 times)

Glory be to the Father*...

(Bow Your Head)
May the Precious Blood that pours out from the Sacred Head of Our
Lord Jesus Christ, the Temple of Divine Wisdom, the Tabernacle of
Divine Knowledge and the Sunshine of Heaven and earth cover us
now and forever. Amen.

L: O Most Precious Blood of Jesus Christ.
**R: Heal the Wounds in the Most Sacred Heart of Jesus. (3
times)**

Hail Holy Queen*...

Let Us Pray
O Most Precious Blood of Jesus Christ, we honor, worship and adore
You because of Your work of the everlasting covenant that brings
peace to mankind. Heal the Wounds in the Most Sacred Heart of
Jesus. Console the Almighty Father in His throne and wash away the
sins of the whole world. May all revere You, O Precious Blood, have
mercy. Amen.

Most Sacred Heart of Jesus	Have mercy on us
Immaculate Heart of Mary	Pray for us
St. Joseph, the husband of Mary	Pray for us
Ss. Peter and Paul	Pray for us
St. John at the foot of the Cross	Pray for us
St. Mary Magdalen	Pray for us
All the prayer warriors and intercessors of Heaven	Pray for us
All the great Saints of Our Lord	Pray for us
All the heavenly hosts	Pray for us
Legion of Mary	Pray for us

LITANY OF THE PRECIOUS BLOOD
OF JESUS CHRIST

Lord, have mercy on us	Lord, have mercy on us
Christ, have mercy on us	Christ, have mercy on us
Lord, have mercy on us	Lord, have mercy on us
Christ, hear us	Christ, graciously hear us
God, the Father of Heaven,	have mercy on us
God the Son, Redeemer of the world,	have mercy on us
God, the Holy Spirit,	have mercy on us
Holy Trinity, One God,	have mercy on us

L: O Most Precious Blood of Jesus Christ, the Blood of Salvation
R: Cover us and the whole world.

The ocean of the Blood of Jesus Christ-   set us free

The Blood of Jesus Christ,
full of holiness and compassion-   set us free

Precious Blood of Jesus Christ, our strength and power- set us free

Precious Blood of Jesus Christ,
the Everlasting Covenant-   set us free

Precious Blood of Jesus Christ,
the Foundation of the Christian faith-   set us free

Precious Blood of Jesus Christ, the Armor of God-   set us free

Precious Blood of Jesus Christ, the Divine Charity-   set us free

Precious Blood of Jesus Christ, the Scourge of Demons- set us free

Precious Blood of Jesus Christ,
the Help of those in bondage-   set us free

Precious Blood of Jesus Christ, the Sacred Wine-   set us free

Precious Blood of Jesus Christ, the Power of Christians- set us free

Precious Blood of Jesus Christ,
the Defender of the Catholic Wall-   set us free

Precious Blood of Jesus Christ,
the Christian's True Faith-   set us free

Precious Blood of Jesus Christ, the Healing Blood-   save us

Precious Blood of Jesus Christ, the Anointing Blood-   save us

Precious Blood of Jesus Christ,
the Boldness of the Children of God-   save us

Precious Blood of Jesus Christ,
the Commander of Christian warriors-   save us

Precious Blood of Jesus Christ, the Blood of Resurrection- save us

Precious Blood of Jesus Christ,
the Drink of heavenly Angels-   save us

Precious Blood of Jesus Christ,
the Consolation of God the Father-   save us

Precious Blood of Jesus Christ,
the Power of the Holy Spirit-   save us

Precious Blood of Jesus Christ,
the Circumcision of the Gentiles-   save us

Precious Blood of Jesus Christ, the Peace of the world-   save us

Precious Blood of Jesus Christ,
the Sunshine of Heaven and earth-   save us

Precious Blood of Jesus Christ, the Rainbow in Heaven-   save us

Precious Blood of Jesus Christ,
the Hope of innocent children-   save us

Precious Blood of Jesus Christ,
the Word of God in our hearts-   save us

Precious Blood of Jesus Christ, the Heavenly Weapon-   save us

Precious Blood of Jesus Christ, the Divine Wisdom-   save us

Precious Blood of Jesus Christ,
the Foundation of the world-   save us

Precious Blood of Jesus Christ,
the Mercy of God the Father-   save us

L: O Most Precious Blood of Jesus Christ
R: Cleanse the sins of the world

L: O Most Precious Blood of Jesus Christ
R: Refine the world

L: O Most Precious Blood of Jesus Christ
R: Teach us how to console Jesus

Let Us Pray

O Precious Blood of our salvation, we believe, hope and trust in You. Deliver all those that are in the hands of the infernal spirits we beseech You. Protect the dying against the works of evil spirits and welcome them into Your eternal glory. Have mercy on the whole world and strengthen us to worship and console the Sacred Heart. We adore you, O Precious Blood of mercy. Amen.

L: O Most Precious Blood of Jesus Christ
R: Heal the wounds in the Most Sacred Heart of Jesus.
(3 times)

Hymn
(Music on page 99)
Blood of Jesus
Blood of Jesus
Blood of Jesus, cover us (3 times)

Adoration Precious Blood of Jesus
Adoration Precious Blood of Jesus Christ

We adore You Precious Blood of Jesus
We adore You Precious Blood of Jesus Christ

Adoration Precious Blood of Jesus
Adoration Precious Blood of Jesus Christ

CONSECRATION TO THE
PRECIOUS BLOOD OF JESUS CHRIST

Conscious, merciful Savior, of my nothingness and of Thy sublimity, I cast myself at Thy Feet and thank Thee for the many proofs of Thy grace shown to me, Thy ungrateful creature. I thank Thee especially for delivering me by Thy Precious Blood from the destructive power of Satan. In the presence of my dear Mother Mary, my guardian Angel, my patron Saint, and of the whole company of Heaven, I dedicate myself voluntarily, with a sincere heart, O dearest Jesus, to Thy Precious Blood, by which Thou hast redeemed the world from sin, death and Hell. I promise Thee, with the help of Thy grace and to the utmost of my strength, to stir up and foster devotion to Thy Precious Blood, the Price of our redemption, so that Thy adorable Blood may be honored and glorified by all. In this way, I wish to make reparation for my disloyalty towards Thy Precious Blood of love, and to make satisfaction to Thee for the many profanations which men commit against that Precious Price of their salvation. O would that my own sins, my coldness, and all the acts of disrespect I have ever committed against Thee, O Holy, Precious Blood, could be undone. Behold, O dearest Jesus, I offer to Thee the love, honor and adoration, which Thy most Holy Mother, Thy faithful disciples and all the Saints have offered to Thy Precious Blood. I ask Thee to forget my earlier faithlessness and coldness, and to forgive all who offend Thee. Sprinkle me, O Divine Savior, and all men with Thy Precious Blood, so that we, O Crucified Love, may love Thee from now on with all our hearts, and worthily honor the Price of our salvation. Amen.

We fly to your patronage, O Holy Mother of God. Despise not our petitions in our necessities, but deliver us from all dangers, O ever Glorious and Blessed Virgin. Amen.

For All Benefactors of this devotion
Our Father*...Hail Mary*...Glory Be*...

CONSOLATION PRAYERS
To the Agonizing Jesus Christ
(23 June 1997)

(1) PRAYER:
Eternal Father, when You were about to send Your only-begotten Son, Our Lord Jesus Christ, into the world with the aim of saving us and bringing a new paradise into the world through the Most Precious Blood, out of love You said, "Whom shall I send, who will go to redeem My people?" The heavenly court was silent until Your Son answered, "Here I am, send Me Father."

Honor and adoration be unto You O Divine Love; praise and worship be unto Your Name, O Loving Jesus Christ. Take consolation, O Agonizing Jesus Christ. The reward You received from Your people for Your benevolence, was sin. They sinned and blasphemed day and night against Your Holy Name. They fought against You and disobeyed Your commandments.

Father, be comforted through the voice of Your heavenly choirs. May the voice of Your Dominions console You. Amen.

Our Father*...Hail Mary*...Glory Be*...

Agonizing Jesus Christ	Bear it Lord
Agonizing Jesus Christ	We love you
Agonizing Heart of Jesus Christ	Your Kingdom come

Hymn
(Music on page 97)
Be consoled O Jesus Christ Our Lord
Your Precious Blood
Shed for us all
Will never be in vain, we pray.

(2) PRAYER:
Eternal Father, You prepared a Holy Tabernacle, the womb of the

Blessed Virgin Mary, for Your only-begotten Son, Jesus Christ. Blessed be the womb which bore the only Son of God.

Father, Your begotten Son was born in Bethlehem and laid in a manger because there was no room in the inn for Him and His parents. It was so that the world will seek the Kingdom of Heaven rather than the perishable wealth of this world.

Father, this indicated that Your own people were not ready to welcome their King, Redeemer and Creator. There was no room for the King of Heaven and Earth in His own land.

Lord, You came to Your own people and they did not recognize You as a King. You came to your own country and they did not know You. When they heard of You they planned for Your death. With that plan, they killed numerous children. A bitter cry and lamentation was echoing in Your own land as a welcome for the King. Women refused to be comforted because their children were dead.

Jesus, You bore all these things for the love You have for Your people. But Your people continued sinning and doing all kinds of evil against You and Your Heavenly Father. As a King, they regarded You as their enemy. As a Redeemer, You were a predator to Your own people whom You saved. Who will, in remembering Your mercy and kindness to Your people, console You enough?

Take consolation. Be comforted, O loving Jesus Christ. May the voice of Your heavenly Choirs of Angels and Archangels praise You and console You. Amen.

Our Father*...Hail Mary*...Glory Be*...

Agonizing Jesus Christ   Bear it Lord
Agonizing Jesus Christ   We love you
Agonizing Heart of Jesus Christ   Your Kingdom come

Hymn
(Music on page 97)
Calm the heat of Your anger, O Lord
We are sorry
We all have sinned
We will never sin again.

(3) PRAYER:

O loving Jesus Christ, You, Who came into the world to redeem Your people from sin. Oh, the Chief Shepherd Who was treated badly and scornfully by His flock. You came and saw Your people defiling the Holy Temple of Your Father. Your fury caused their being chased out of the Holy Temple. And today, men are becoming most carnal by neglecting Your presence in the Holy Tabernacle.

We console You for the sins men commit against You in the Holy Tabernacle, for the coldness and neglect which they show in Your presence, for those who receive You unworthily, and for all the acts of disrespect which men commit against You. Forgive, pardon, O Loving Jesus Christ.

Although men crucify You again and again, in Your great mercy bear all these insults from Your beloved creatures. O merciful Jesus Christ, accept our consolation, we pray You, and have mercy on Your people. May the voice of the heavenly Virtues console You. Amen.

Our Father*…Hail Mary*…Glory Be*…

Agonizing Jesus Christ	Bear it Lord
Agonizing Jesus Christ	We love you
Agonizing Heart of Jesus Christ	Your Kingdom come

Hymn
(Music on page 97)
Agonizing Heart of Jesus Christ
You have suffered
And paid for our lives
May Your Will be done on Earth.

(4) PRAYER:
O Merciful and Loving Jesus Christ, You suffered sorrowfully and fearfully in the Garden of Gethsemane. Thus You said, "My soul is sorrowful, even unto death." We console Your Sacred Heart which bears much pain. You suffered scourging at the pillar and crowning with thorns for us to be reconciled with God. Nevertheless, many innocent souls are being aborted daily and their cries wound Your Sacred Heart. We pray You to forgive men all their trespasses.

May the voices of the heavenly Cherubim and Seraphim console You, and may the tone of the evangelization of this world comfort You. Amen.

Our Father*…Hail Mary*…Glory Be*…

Agonizing Jesus Christ	Bear it Lord
Agonizing Jesus Christ	We love you
Agonizing Heart of Jesus Christ	Your Kingdom come

Hymn
(Music on page 97)
Jesus in the Holy Eucharist
We are sorry
For all the sins
Committed against You on Earth

(5) PRAYER:
O Good and Merciful Jesus Christ, Who offered yourself as a Sacrificial Lamb for the salvation of mankind, we console You. In humility You surrendered to the Jewish soldiers who dragged You like a criminal, mercilessly to the merciless, O Good God, to be judged by man. We console You, O Agonizing Jesus Christ, for all these insults received in the world's courts. We console You for all the cruel torments You suffered from Your people. May You be adored forever. Amen.

L: Adoration to the Wounds in Your Sacred Body.

R: Take consolation, O Most Sacred Heart, who bears all these pains.

L: Adoration to Your Sacred Head who bears the shameful Crown of Thorns.
R: We console You, O Most Sacred Heart, who bears all these pains.

L: Adoration to the Two Hearts of Love that met on the way to Calvary.
R: Accept our consolation, O Hearts of Mother and Son. We offer you consolation for all the anguish and grief You suffered on the way to Calvary.

L: Adoration to Your Most Precious Blood shed on the streets of Jerusalem.
R: Receive consolation Lord, for Your Blood served as the atonement. On Calvary the Creator of Heaven and Earth stood naked in the sight of all men.

L: Adoration to You, Agonizing Jesus Christ, Who bears this shame for the remission of the sins of the world.
R: Glory, honor and adoration be Yours Who humbly accepted the Cross of my salvation. On lying on the Cross, the soldiers straightened You and nailed Your hands and Feet. Honor and adoration to Your Sacred Wounds and Your Most Precious mingled Blood. We pray You, bear all these great pains and sorrows You suffered on the Cross.

L: Adoration to Your Holy Death, Spotless Lamb of God.
R: Reign forever, O Most Precious Blood and Water from Your Sacred Side. O Agonizing Jesus Christ, Your Kingdom come! Amen.

Our Father*...Hail Mary*...Glory Be*...

Agonizing Jesus Christ   Bear it Lord
Agonizing Jesus Christ   We love you
Agonizing Heart of Jesus Christ   Your Kingdom come

Hymn
(Music on page 97)
Crucified Jesus Christ on the Cross
Drops of Your Blood
Were all counted
For us all to meditate

L: Agonizing Jesus Christ, the only Son of God, Redeemer and Creator of the world, forgive and have mercy on the whole world.
R: Agonizing Heart of Jesus Christ, receive consolation. Amen. (3 times)

ADORATION PRAYERS
To the Most Precious Blood of Jesus Christ

Almighty and Eternal Father, the magnitude of Your love for us is reflected fully in the gift of Your only-begotten Son to humanity. He is not only equal to You but one with You. We are indebted to You and it stares us in the face. Obviously, we cannot pay You commensurately. But we are asking for Your grace while demonstrating our willingness to love You in this adoration. We appreciate Your benevolence and solicit Your continued loving kindness in helping us to put forth a more satisfying gesture of love and gratefulness through a change of our lives for the better.

May the Holy Archangel Michael with Your Hosts of Angels and Saints join us and lead us closer to you through this adoration. We make this prayer through Christ Our Lord. Amen.

Our Father*...Hail Mary*...Glory Be*...

Hymn
(Music on page 99)
Adoration Precious Blood of Jesus
Adoration Precious Blood of Jesus Christ

We adore You, Precious Blood of Jesus
We adore You, Precious Blood of Jesus Christ

Adoration Precious Blood of Jesus
Adoration Precious Blood of Jesus Christ

(1) PRAYER:

O Loving Jesus Christ, Whose mercy is endless, we adore Your Agonizing Heart which bears great pains and sorrows for the salvation of man; Divine Lamb of God, Son of God and Son of the Virgin Mary, God and Man. You who suffered sorrowfully for the love of mankind; Who in great fear and anguish sweated blood in the Garden of Gethsemane, we adore Your Most Precious Blood and the sorrow in Your Agonizing Heart. We beg You for Your Holy Church, the Pope, the Cardinals, Bishops, Clergy, and non-clergy who are under the shade of Your Most Precious Blood, protection, peace and love, so that through the intercession of St. Michael and all the Archangels of Heaven, we might conquer the Red Dragon. Amen.

Our Father*...Hail Mary*...Glory Be*...

Hymn
(Music on page 97)
Jesus in the Holy Eucharist
May the time come
That You prayed for
When we may be one in You.

(If possible touch forehead to ground, or bow)
May the Most Precious Blood that pours out from the Sacred Head of Our Lord Jesus Christ, the Temple of Divine Wisdom, the Tabernacle of Divine Knowledge, and the Sunshine of Heaven and Earth,

cover us now and forever. Amen.
L: O Most Precious Blood of Jesus Christ
R: Adoration and praise be Yours forever. Amen.

(2) PRAYER:
O loving Jesus Christ, Whose mercy is endless, we adore Your Agonizing Heart which bears great pains and sorrows for the salvation of
man. Gentle Lamb of God, Son of God and Son of the Virgin Mary,
God and Man, You allowed Your Sacred Body to be tied and scourged
at the pillar in order to free us from sin and bring salvation to mankind. We adore Your Most Precious Blood from the numerous Wounds
in Your Sacred Body. We pray for the conversion of unrepentant sinners in the whole world. May You allow a drop of Your Blood to fall
on their hearts, so that through the intercession of the Cherubim and
Seraphim and all Angels of Heaven, all men will turn to You. Amen.

Our Father*...Hail Mary*...Glory Be*...

Hymn
(Music on page 97)
Agonizing Heart of Jesus Christ
We adore You
And give You praise
May all honour be to You.

(If possible touch forehead to ground, or bow)
May the Most Precious Blood that pours out from the Sacred Head
of Our Lord Jesus Christ, the Temple of Divine Wisdom, the Tabernacle of Divine Knowledge, and the Sunshine of Heaven and Earth,
cover us now and forever. Amen.
L: O Most Precious Blood of Jesus Christ
R: Adoration and praise be Yours forever. Amen.

(3) PRAYER:
O Loving Jesus Christ, Whose mercy is endless, we adore Your Agonizing Heart which bears great pains and sorrows for the salvation of
man. O Most meek Lamb of God, Son of God and Son of the Virgin

Mary, God and Man, Your Sacred Head was crowned with thorns. The Temple of Divine Wisdom was beaten by reckless sinners with iron rods in order to bring peace to the world and evolve a New Garden of Eden.

We adore the Most Precious Blood which oozes from Your Sacred Head. We implore You for the liberation of the souls in Purgatory, and the protection of dying souls. Pour out Your Precious Blood that all Your enemies will be scattered through the intercession of the Thrones and Powers of Heaven and all its hosts. Amen.

Our Father*...Hail Mary*...Glory Be*...

Hymn
(Music on page 97)
Jesus in the Holy Eucharist
As we adore You
We praise Your Name
And rely on You for peace.

(If possible touch forehead to ground, or bow)
May the Most Precious Blood that pours out from the Sacred Head of Our Lord Jesus Christ, the Temple of Divine Wisdom, the Tabernacle of Divine Knowledge, and the Sunshine of Heaven and Earth, cover us now and forever. Amen.
L: O Most Precious Blood of Jesus Christ
R: Adoration and praise be Yours forever. Amen.

(4) PRAYER:
O Loving Jesus Christ, Whose mercy is endless, we adore Your Agonizing Heart which bears great pains and sorrows for the salvation of man. Spotless Lamb of God, Son of God and Son of the Virgin Mary, God and Man, in Humility You received the Cross of Salvation and made Your way to Calvary. There, You sprinkled Your Precious Blood on the streets of Jerusalem. We adore Your sprinkled Most Precious Blood.

We beg for the release of those in captivity and for the return of non-Catholics into the One, Holy, Catholic and Apostolic Church founded by You. Sprinkle Your Most Precious Blood that by the intercession of Your Heavenly Dominions and all the Angels, captives shall be freed and lost sheep will come back under one flock. Amen.

Our Father*...Hail Mary*...Glory Be*...

Hymn
(Music on page 97)
Agonizing Heart of Jesus Christ
Praise and honour
Be unto You
Please make all hearts turn to You

(If possible touch forehead to ground, or bow)
May the Most Precious Blood that pours out from the Sacred Head of Our Lord Jesus Christ, the Temple of Divine Wisdom, the Tabernacle of Divine Knowledge, and the Sunshine of Heaven and Earth, cover us now and forever. Amen.
L: O Most Precious Blood of Jesus Christ
R: Adoration and praise be Yours forever. Amen.

(5) PRAYER:
O Loving Jesus Christ Whose mercy is endless, we adore Your Agonizing Heart which bears great pains and sorrows for the salvation of man. Merciful Lamb of God, Son of God and Son of the Virgin Mary, God and Man, in humility You accepted the Cross of the Salvation of the world. You humbly straightened Your Body on the Cross, while Your own people held You and nailed You to it. We adore Your Most Precious Blood which pours out from Your Hands and Feet. We beg You to protect the living saints in the whole world against the activities of the Antichrist. Pour Your Most Precious Blood on them, that by the intercession of the Virtues and all the Angels, they will end their struggles in Heaven. Amen.

Our Father*...Hail Mary*...Glory Be*...

Hymn
(Music on page 97)
Let us sing with you Virgin Mother
And love with you
Your Son Our Lord
Jesus Christ Who died for us.

(If possible touch forehead to ground, or bow)
May the Most Precious Blood that pours out from the Sacred Head
of Our Lord Jesus Christ, the Temple of Divine Wisdom, the Tabernacle of Divine Knowledge, and the Sunshine of Heaven and Earth,
cover us now and forever. Amen.
L: O Most Precious Blood of Jesus Christ
R: Adoration and praise be Yours forever. Amen.

(6) PRAYER:
O Loving Jesus Christ, Whose mercy is endless, we adore Your Agonizing Heart which bears great pains and sorrows for the salvation of
man. Sacrificial Lamb, Son of God and Son of the Virgin Mary, God
and Man, the wicked men of the world pierced Your Sacred Side.
Blood and Water mingled and flowed which washed and saved the
world from sin.

We adore You, O Most Precious Blood and Water; we implore You to
save the life of every innocent unborn child and baptize aborted children with the Water from Your Sacred Side, in the Name of the Father, and of the Son, and of the Holy Spirit. May they through the
intercession of the Principalities of Heaven and all the Angels reach
the everlasting home. Amen.

Our Father*...Hail Mary*...Glory Be*...

Hymn
(Music on page 97)
Agonizing Heart of Jesus Christ
We adore You
And give You thanks
And praise You forever more.

(If possible touch forehead to ground, or bow)
May the Most Precious Blood that pours out from the Sacred Head
of Our Lord Jesus Christ, the Temple of Divine Wisdom, the Tabernacle of Divine Knowledge, and the Sunshine of Heaven and Earth,
cover us now and forever. Amen.
L: O Most Precious Blood of Jesus Christ
R: Adoration and praise be Yours forever. Amen.

(7) PRAYER:
O Loving Jesus Christ, Whose mercy is endless, how can we express
our love for You? You made Your Most Precious Blood the drink of
the Heavenly Angels. We praise You, O Most Precious Blood. We
worship You, O Most Precious Blood. We adore You, O Most Precious Blood. All creatures adore the Most Precious Blood. Amen.

Hymn
(Music on page 97)
Glory and thanks be to the Father
Honor and praise
To His Son, Christ
And to the Spirit Divine

L: Adoration to You, O Most Precious Blood of Jesus Christ
R: The Blood of Salvation

L: Adoration to You, O Most Precious Blood of Jesus Christ
R: The Everlasting Covenant

L: Adoration to You, O Most Precious Blood of Jesus Christ
R: The Heavenly Weapon

L: Adoration to You, O Most Precious Blood of Jesus Christ
R: The Hope of innocent children

L: Adoration to You, O Most Precious Blood of Jesus Christ
R: The Consolation of God the Father. Amen.

THE ANGUISHED APPEALS
Reparation Prayers to the Agonizing Jesus Christ
(10 December 1998)

Lord Jesus Christ, throughout history You are leading us back to the Almighty Father. We are immensely grateful. We appreciate Your love. We remember, with heartfelt sorrow, our weaknesses, sins, and all Your suffering in this noble task. Can we lessen it? We pray You, help us to do it by our style of life. Henceforth, we shall do whatever is required if only You will it. Show us more love by willing it. We make this prayer in the Name of Jesus Christ Our Lord, Who lives and reigns with the Father, in the unity of the Holy Spirit, one God forever and ever. Amen.

Short and Efficacious Reparation Prayer
to the Eternal Father
(22 July 1999)

("All who adore My Precious Blood, console My Father Who loves His Son the most. As you adore My Precious Blood, the pains of My Sacred Heart are lessened. The Sorrowful Heart of My Mother will also be consoled. Children, adore My Precious Blood always and offer it to My Father for mercy. Hear this prayer. Pray it always in reparation for the sins of the world. Pray it three times; each time you pray it, I assure you the Divine Mercy will multiply. Pray it always and many times a day, since you are living in ungodly days. Pray it so that you shall be safe from the purification fire. Children, make it known to the whole world.")

Eternal Father, I offer You all the Wounds of Your dearly beloved Son, Jesus Christ, the pains and agonies of His Most Sacred Heart and His Most Precious Blood, which gushed forth from all His Wounds, in reparation for my sins and those of the whole world. Amen. (3 times)

Apostle's Creed*... (Brief silence)...

THE FIRST ANGUISHED APPEAL

Where are you, my son? Your Master is looking for you. Come to me! Come nearer and hear My agonizing appeal.

My son, there once was a Man who had many sheep. He looked after them and shepherded them well. Whenever they were thirsty, He led them to a spring of flowing water to satisfy their thirst. He did not allow them to feel hungry. He led them to a beautiful green pasture. They ate and grew fat and strong. The Man fortified the pasture land so that no wolf would enter to harm the flock.

One day, the sheep planned a rebellion and forcefully escaped from the camp and entered the forest. There, they were captured by wild animals. They were like slaves without hope. Their bodies and blood were used for festivals and animal sacrifices to their gods. Nevertheless, the Man did not forget His flock. He sent all His servants and they were killed. Lastly, He sent His Son Who eventually won the battle.

The Son of Man led the flock shepherdly day and night in the wilderness. On their way, they underwent many difficulties which they could not withstand. They complained to the Son of Man, uttered all kinds of cruel words against Him, and finally killed Him. Son, when the Father of the Son of Man hears about the death of His Son, what do you think He will do?

(Silence)

My son, you and your people are the flock. My Father is the owner of the flock Who sent many prophets to His people who are living in this terrifying wilderness. I am the Son Whom you persecuted and killed. What have I done to you? Despite all your sinful acts, My Father is still calling you to return to Him. But you pay no attention to His call. RETURN! O Israel My people! Make reparation for the sins you and the whole world commit against My Father and against My Precious Blood. I am the Agonizing Jesus Christ.

(Silence)

My God, my God*...Act of Contrition*...Our Father*...Hail Mary* ...
Glory Be*(3 times)...

Hymn
(Music on page 97)
Agonizing Jesus Christ Our Lord
You have suffered
And paid for our life
May Your Will be done on Earth.

Calm the heat of Your anger O Lord
We are sorry
We all have sinned
We will never sin again.

Jesus in the Holy Eucharist
When You called us
We knew nothing
Forgive us we pray O Lord.

Prayer to the Most Holy Trinity*...Agonizing Prayer*...

SECOND ANGUISHED APPEAL

My son, come closer to Me, hear My anguished appeal. For love of you I offer My Body as a living sacrifice – a bread of life for all men. My Blood is a precious drink – the drink of heavenly Angels lovingly given to men.

My son, I remain for you in the Sacrament of Love waiting for you patiently in the Tabernacle where I am in prison for you. You rarely approach Me because you do not remember Me Who am in prison for you. My son, My agony is great when I see the coldness, the mindlessness and neglect with which you approach the Holy Trinity,

Whose presence fills the Holy Sanctuary. I am here, my son. I am here in fullness. Fear the presence of your God, approach with respect and awe.

My son, do you know what I suffer whenever I enter the sanctuary of your heart through Holy Communion? Your sins tie me up and beat Me mercilessly. In your heart there is no one to console Me. After callously scourging Me, you drag Me away and lock up the door of your heart with iniquity. This is what you do to Me with your sinful life. I am the Bread of Life for all men who receive Me in a state of sanctity. I come to give you life not death. Clean the iniquities of your heart. Open the door of your heart for Me. Make your heart a tabernacle of consolation for Me. Son, may I live in your sanctuary from one Communion to the other. Welcome Me, welcome Me, My son. All who welcome Me, welcome My Father and the Holy Spirit Who live in Me. All who reject Me, reject the Holy Trinity. Son, even if others will reject Me, make your heart a tabernacle of My consolation.

I am the Agonizing Jesus Christ, calling you to RETURN.

(Silence)

My God, my God*...Act of Contrition*...Our Father*...Hail Mary* ...
Glory Be* (3 times)...

Hymn #1
(Music on page 100)
The awareness of Christ's Passion
Helps the heart of man turn to God
When everything fails but God's grace.
May we be solely Yours.

What feeling now do you have
Thinking of the sins of the world?
May we know the pains we cause You
For going against Your Will.

May we feel the way You feel Lord
May we pray the way You pray Lord
May we feel the way You feel Lord
We want to live for You.

Prayer to the Most Holy Trinity*...Agonizing Prayer*...

THIRD ANGUISHED APPEAL

My son, I am in your heart, a lonely Gethsemane, where I am watching and no one dares to come and watch with Me even for one hour. You would rather chase the possession of earthly wealth even at the risk of perdition, leaving Me alone to suffer. The enemy is fast approaching; he is gaining ground so as to win many souls while you are asleep. Son, can't you wake up and watch with Me even one hour? I am in the sanctuary of your soul, a lonely Gethsemane, waiting for you to come.

Many souls, many souls are going to Hell because of the sins of the flesh. Son, see how you keep on leading many souls to perdition through your fashions. I am the one Whom you publicly expose naked. Son, console Me. Son, have mercy on Me. Never should a man imitate a woman! Never should a woman imitate a man! Be what I made you, son; be what I made you. I say, keep away from this worldly fashion. This is the plan of the enemy to destroy the temple of the Holy Spirit; that is your body. Live a modest life.

My loving son, because I love you and want you to show Me love, I am appealing to you to offer Me your whole being, keeping it for Me and for Me alone. May it glorify Me always, may it console Me always. I am not making this appeal to the world, but to you whom I love. Offer it to Me, offer it for salvation. I am the Agonizing Jesus Christ, calling you to RETURN.

(Silence)

My God, my God*...Act of Contrition*... Our Father*...Hail

Mary* …
Glory Be* (3 times)…

Hymn #2
(Music on page 101)
Seeing the sins people do commit in the world
I ask you to have mercy and forgive.
Thinking of my own sins and the sins of the world,
I plead for Divine Mercy.

Christ was nailed on the cross to detach us from sin
What effort are you making to appreciate
He was on Calvary to send us to Heaven
O what a loving Father.

Whatever cross You deem right for me to behold
I accept it whole heartedly my Lord
May Your Precious Blood,
Give me the strength and the grace
To Triumph in all trials.

Prayer to the Most Holy Trinity*… Agonizing Prayer*…

FOURTH ANGUISHED APPEAL

My son, is this how you betray your Master and Savior? Only because of worldly money which perishes in this earthly life that you choose to betray your Master and hand Me over to the cruel men who crucify Me. Son, you are making yourself the Judas of the last age. For how terrible it will be for those who betray the Son of God, who hand Him over to sinful men to be crucified. See how they will regrettably pass into eternity and suffer eternally. Even among the priests of my heart, there are many Judases who choose worldly possessions in exchange for their Master Who is in agony.

This pains me much, My son, for they are making My Father's house a market place. My Father is greatly annoyed. Look and see how you are chasing Me away from My Holy sanctuary. Son, do you want the presence of your God? Offer Me your life. I am the one Whom you are betraying only because of these earthly things. Son, since all these things you are laboring for will be destroyed by fire, why are you laboring in vain? Return to Me My son. Have mercy on He Who came to save. Let My priests return to Me. I am the Agonizing Jesus Christ Who loves you, appealing to you to RETURN.

(Silence)

**My God, my God*...Act of Contrition*...Our Father*...Hail Mary* ...
Glory Be* (3 times)...**

Hymn
(Music on page 97)
I have sinned against the Lord my God
I am sorry
I beg pardon
Forgive me I pray You Lord

You are merciful to me O Lord
May I show You
The same mercy
By living as You on earth.

Refine and accept our souls O Lord
You bled much
To save mankind
Bid all souls return to You.

Prayer to the Most Holy Trinity*... Agonizing Prayer*...

FIFTH ANGUISHED APPEAL

My son, when will the torments of My scourging due to your sins and those of the world end? Why are you scourging Me and at the same time crowning Me with thorns? And thus saying, **"Let me sin, afterwards I will go to Confession."** I am the Agonizing Jesus Christ Whom you constantly torture. **Son, did I give you the Sacrament of Penance for you to become a swine of iniquity?** This is the Sacrament of My Love. It opens up the ocean of Divine Mercy, the Precious Blood and Water which gushed out to save and cleanse your iniquity, so that you will go and sin no more.

Son, withdraw the crown of thorns, Have mercy on Me, scourge Me not again. Love your God your Creator. Have no other gods of any creature. Only your God shall you fear and worship. Call not the name of your God in vain. Son, remember to keep the day of obligation holy. Prove My Name in this bribery-filled and corrupt world. Have all these things done so as to lessen the pains of My agony. Offer all your disappointments, trials, and persecutions in atonement for your sins and those of the whole world. I am the Agonizing Jesus Christ, pleading with you to RETURN.

(Silence)

My God, my God*...Act of Contrition*...Our Father*...Hail Mary* ...
Glory Be* (3 times)...

Hymn #1
(Music on page 100)
Teach me to observe Your laws, O Lord
I will keep them with all my heart.
Your Will is embodied therein
I want to do Your Will

As we receive You in the Eucharist
May we give You ourselves in return
For Your gift of self is our life
May we remain grateful.

Rectify your lives as Christians
Check the way you live with your God
Seek for Him Who loves you always
He wants to save us all.

Prayer to the Most Holy Trinity*... Agonizing Prayer*...

SIXTH ANGUISHED APPEAL

My son, draw closer to Me and hear My anguished appeal. I am daily looking for someone to console Me and find none. Look at My Agonizing Face. Where is the Veronica of the last age? Where is she who will wipe My Bloody Face and console Me? Is she the one who joins the multitude in saying, "Crucify Him! Crucify Him!"? They have forgotten that I am their Messiah Who brought them out of Egypt, Who fed them with heavenly manna and shepherded them under My wings in the dry and hot desert. You have rejected Me and there is no one to help Me.

Son, this is how you abandoned your cross and turned away from the way of Calvary, leaving Me alone to suffer. **Verily, I say to you My son, there is no other way which can lead to the land of promise other than the road of the Holy Cross.** *Carry your cross and follow Me all the days of your life.* Help Me to carry all these rejected crosses which My people have abandoned for Me to carry. **Son, live the life of your consecration.** Carry your cross and follow Me. I am the Agonizing Jesus Christ Who is calling you to RETURN.

(Silence)

**My God, my God*...Act of Contrition*...Our Father*...Hail Mary* ...
Glory Be* (3 times)...**

Hymn #2
(Music on page 101)
Thinking of the way Christ died on the cross for our sins
Sorrow for sin fills our hearts and we say
Pardon your people who sinned and say they are sorry
We will never sin again

O Lord Who breathed to give us life in this world
And breathed Your last to save us from death
May Your Holy breath never be in vain, we pray Lord
Save us from eternal death.

Agonizing Jesus Who has paid for our souls
We are grateful to You and say bear it
We can never be grateful enough for Your gifts
May You reign forever more.

Prayer to the Most Holy Trinity*... Agonizing Prayer*...

SEVENTH ANGUISHED APPEAL

My Son, look up and see how your sins hang Me on the Cross. I am bleeding for love of you. I am sweating for love of you. I am thirsty for love of this needful world. None of you is willing to console Me, rather you offer Me vinegar when I am thirsty. You all stand afar, mock and criticize Me. My son, see how you are speaking falsely against your neighbor. Instead of praying for my Holy Church, you stand out criticizing it. I am the Agonizing Jesus Christ Whom you are criticizing. The Church is My Body Whom you are crucifying.

My son, stand at the foot of My Holy Cross and offer, with My Mother, the whole world to Me. I will accept them and offer them to My Father. They will be His sons and daughters, and obey His commands. The wrath of the Eternal Father will be calmed; My Holy Wounds will be healed. Then My Kingdom will come on earth. Son, have yourself crucified for Me and with Me on the Holy Cross of Salvation. This is what I mostly need of you in atonement for your sins and those of the whole world. Son, I did not appeal for these things to the world, but to you, because I love you and I want you to show Me love.

I promise to draw all men with you to Myself through you. Accept My Anguished Appeal, O My loving son. I will offer all your sacrifices that will be acceptable to God in reparation for your sins and those of the whole world. In the end, the whole world will live in Me, with me and for Me. My Sacred Side will be opened for all men as a refuge. They will draw the Living Water from the Fountain of Life that pours out from My Sacred Side. Son, let My Will be done on earth. Let My Will be done in you. Suffer for Me and with Me. Die for Me and live in Me. I am the Agonizing Jesus Christ. I love you. I bless you all.

(Silence)

My God, my God*...Act of Contrition*...Our Father*...Hail Mary* ...
Glory Be* (3 times)...

Hymn #2
(Music on page 101)
Would that we had cost you less than we did, O Lord
We would have been happier than we are now
When we call to mind all You have suffered for us
We say sorry, pardon us

May the grace of Your Agonizing Heart be for us
Source of true love and pure heart, Lord Jesus.
All we are and all we have all come from You Lord
They are all Your gifts to us.

May our comfort never be Your discomfort Lord
When we look for comfort, please take the lead
It is Your Commandments that give light to our steps
What You sanction, that we do

Prayer to the Most Holy Trinity*... Agonizing Prayer*...

(Bow your head)
Glory Be* (7 times)...

THE MYSTICAL PRAYERS
Of Our Lord Jesus Christ

(These prayers, revealed by Our Lord as His petitions to His Heavenly Father during His Passion, were dictated to Barnabas for us to pray daily.)

Prayer to Vanquish Satan and his Agents
(5 July 1998)

("There is no need for you to fear those numerous populations of the enemy. Children, simply offer the Wounds, Pains and Blood of My left Hand for their downfall; you will see them disappear like ashes...I assure you, many kingdoms of the enemy will disappear in the twinkle of an eye. Pray it and teach it to all men. My Precious Blood will save.")

All you great number of enemies of the Holy Death of my Master Jesus Christ on the Cross of Calvary, the prince of darkness and iniquity, the father of all liars, I stand on the death of my Master Jesus Christ and offer His pains, Wounds, and the Precious Blood from His left Hand to the Eternal Father for your downfall, your destruction and your scourging. Amen. **Precious Blood of my Master Jesus Christ - reign in me and in the lives of all men. Amen.**

Prayer for the Protection and Unity of the Flock
(6 July 1998)

("My children, whenever you say this prayer you are making the hour of my Kingdom on earth come sooner. Through this prayer My Father will let it come down soon; the hour of the Second Pentecost, when My prayer will be fulfilled that all shall be one...All who carry out this devotion will rejoice greatly when My Kingdom comes. I will protect them always.")

Eternal Father, I offer You all the Wounds, pains, and the Precious Blood from the Sacred Feet of Your Son, Our Lord and Master, for all Your children who are wondering like sheep without a shepherd in this terrifying forest. Protect them against wild predators and give them peace that they might be one, and united in the same way as the nail held fast the Feet of my Master and Savior, Jesus Christ. Amen. **Precious Blood of Jesus Christ - reign forever. Amen.**

Prayer for Refuge in the Sacred Side of Jesus Christ
(7 July 1998)

*("My children, these evil days will swallow many souls. That is why I teach this mysterious prayer to you in order that you all might be saved. My Sacred Side is open for **all** men. Pray it and make it known to all men. All who teach this prayer to others will be protected. I love you all. Run for your lives.... ")*

O Loving Father, God of Abraham, Isaac and Jacob, Who protected the Israelites of old in His Holy Wings in the dryness of the cold and hot desert; I offer You the Holy death of my Master and Savior, Jesus Christ, for the protection of Your people who are scattered all over the world. May the Blood and Water wash and strengthen, save and cleanse us that we might find home in the Sacred Side of Your Son which opens for all men. Amen. **Sacred Side of Jesus Christ – be our home for safety. Amen.**

Prayer for Release from Ancestral Curses
(8 July 1998)

("My children, pray it and make it known to the whole world. All who are under curses and constantly say this prayer shall be free from their curses. Any family that is suffering from the curse of sins made by their forefathers, and makes a 144 day novena through this prayer, will be freed. All who break a covenant and who are supposed to die shall be saved and also be released from their curse if they constantly say this prayer and repent.")

Eternal Father, You are the only Immortal God, God Who is love, merciful and kind. Look at Your only-begotten Son, Jesus Christ, and have mercy. I offer You the pains of His scourging at the pillar, His Wounds and Blood for all Your people who are living under the weight of the curse due to the sins of their ancestors and their disobedience for breaking the covenant they made with You. May You set us free through the scourging of Your Son, heal us through His Wounds and save us through His Precious Blood. Amen. **Precious Blood of Jesus Christ – release us from curses. Holy Wounds of Jesus Christ – heal our wounds. By Your scourging – seal us. Amen.**

Prayer for the Sustenance of the Faith
(9 July 1998)

("When I was about to leave My people on earth, My agony grew greater when I remembered their unfaithfulness. I also remembered the period that is coming is terrible and fearful; that many will betray Me like Judas, while others will deny that they know me...Children pray this prayer always for faith and make it known to the whole world before the perilous era comes in full force. If you have little faith, even as small as the mustard seed, you will overcome this period. This mysterious prayer is powerful. Teach it to the whole world. I love you all.")

Omnipotent and Omniscient God, God of Elijah and the prophets, look at the Sacred Head of Your only-begotten Son and have mercy. Arise and save Your people. I offer You all the shame, the pains, the Wounds and the Precious Blood from the Sacred Head of Your Son for all Your children who are living in these perilous times. Strengthen our faith through the mockery of Your Son Jesus Christ and save us through the Precious Blood from His Sacred Head. May we through the sufferings of Your Son Jesus Christ learn to suffer in You and die in You. Amen. **Holy tortures of Jesus Christ – increase our faith. Amen.**

Prayer for the Manifestation of the Divine Will
(10 July 1998)

("My Agony...grew worse and worse when I entered Gethsemane. I looked at my people and saw that they were asleep while their enemy was fast approaching and gaining ground...my Agonizing Heart broke

out with these words "Why are you sleeping, can't you watch with me even one hour? Pray that you will not fall into temptation." When I knelt down again in prayer the burden of my death weighed me down. "Father, take this cup away from me, but not my will, rather yours be done."...Finally, I looked up and prayed to my Father thus...make it known to the whole world for the reign of my Father on earth.")

Eternal Father, You are the Creator and Author of life. You love the world You made. That is why You sent Your only-begotten Son to come for its redemption, so that Your Kingdom will come. Look upon Your Son and rise up in Your throne. Raise Your right Hand and save Your people. I offer You all the sufferings, pains, and death of Your only-begotten Son Whom You love, for Your triumph and reign on earth. May You, through the Precious Blood of Your Son, make a new covenant and bring all Your children back to Your Holy Will. Amen. **Precious Blood of Jesus Christ – reign forever. Agonizing Jesus Christ – Thy Kingdom come. Amen.**

Prayer for Endurance through the Coming Chastisement
(13 July 1998)

("My children pray that this period you are living in now will be shortened. Pray also that your faith will not fail. Be on your guard. Be alert and watch always...How many of you will fight and drive back my adversary, conquer, and bring the captives home?...My children learn this prayer and pray it always especially during the hour of trials...When my people rejected me and condemned me and said "Crucify Him! Crucify Him!" I looked up to heaven and prayed to my Father and said...")

Merciful and Loving Father, Your wish is that all men should be saved. Kindly look on Your rejected and condemned Son Who suffered many tortures and will suffer many tortures through the sins of Your people. Look and see what sin has done to your only-begotten Son. I offer all people who are living in these ungodly and wicked days, all the tortures, pains, rejections, and shame of Your Son Jesus Christ to You, for faith to withstand trials and patience to withstand long tortures. May they through the sufferings of Your only Son fight to the end. Amen. **Our Lord's torture – increase our faith. Precious Blood of Jesus – save us. Amen.**

Prayer for Fallen Sheep and Against a Fall in Faith
(22 July 1998)

(*"I envisaged constant abandonment of faith in my people and how they will constantly reject their God and crucify Me daily. The pains grew in intensity when I saw how hard it will be for them to return...Many there were who would stop on the way because they thought the way was too hard and too long...How large the number of My people who will lose hope and fall...I say to you, My children, wake up and stand firm! During My fall, I remembered all these things and offered them to My Father through this prayer...Through it, My Father will pour on you all the needed graces to endure until the end. All who pray it devotedly will possess the fullness of the Holy Spirit and learn to be obedient and humble."*)

Eternal and Loving Father, look kindly on Your only-begotten Son. See the heavy cross they prepared for Your only Son and have mercy on Your people. I offer You all the pains, sufferings, and the Precious Blood of Your Son Jesus Christ, Emmanuel; for all Your people who have abandoned their faith and will abandon their faith in the mountainous hills and deep valleys of this world. May they through the falling of Your Son under the Cross have strength to rise again and stand firm in the true faith. Through the ocean of His Precious Blood dumped under the Cross on the streets of Jerusalem strengthen all who are eager to do Your Will. Amen. **Precious Blood of Jesus Christ – strengthen our weakened souls. Amen.**

Prayer for the Reign of Glory on Earth
(27 July 1998)

(*"The manifestation of the Red Dragon and the Antichrist in this last hour of this age pierced My Heart greatly during My ministry on earth and even more when I was about to breathe My last on the cross. As I hung on the cross, I envisaged the proud Dragon. It boasted to reign on earth forever...I silently offered My Father this prayer* *for the downfall of the enemy of the cross...My children, through this prayer the Antichrist and the Red Dragon and his agents will have a short hour of reign on earth. **The more you pray, the shorter the hour of their reign on earth.** ")*

O Loving and Merciful Father, all knowing and all powerful, the Alpha and the Omega, the Eternal Father Who created all things, that You should forsake Your children, Your nature forbids. Look kindly on Your begotten Son Jesus Christ Who came to save men and bring Your Kingdom down on earth. We offer You all the agonies, tortures, pains, and the Precious Blood of Your Son Jesus Christ for the defeat of all the enemies of the Holy Cross of Salvation, the Antichrist and the Red Dragon who are fighting against the truth now and in the end of the age. May they, through the Precious Blood of our Redeemer and His last breath on earth, disappear like foam exposed under the sun, so that Your Kingdom may quickly come on earth. Amen. **Precious Blood of Jesus Christ – Thy Kingdom come. Amen.**

Prayer Against the Sins of the Flesh
(28 July 1998)

("Do you know that I was naked in the sight of all men so that you shall defeat and kill the desires of the flesh which lead to this sin of fornication and adultery? Children, my adversary used this sin to claim all men to himself...Any sinner who constantly prays this prayer will gain true repentance...The more you pray it the more many will return to me and leave fornication and adultery. Many people will be lost due to the sins of the flesh. Work hard to save souls...")

Holy and Merciful Father, Your only-begotten Son is standing naked in the sight of all men, so that Your people will know and fear Your Holy Law. Accept my humble prayer for all Your people who are living under iniquity, fornication and adultery, that through all the shame and disgrace of Your only-begotten Son, You will touch their lives for repentance and save them. May they, through the Precious Blood of Your Son Jesus Christ, which I plead to fall on their hearts, gain repentance and be saved and through His shame make them bold for repentance. Amen.

Prayer for the Baptism of Aborted Babies
(29 July 1998)

("Today the blood of innocent children has filled Heaven. Their number is too great, too great; the wrath of the Eternal Father is about to fall on mankind...Their blood disturbs My Agonizing Heart and increases My agony...Through this prayer, large numbers of innocent unborn babies will be saved; pray it daily and make it known to the world. Anyone who teaches it will not be lost. Innocent souls in Heaven will not let them become lost. I, with My Love and Mercy, will protect them from falling into mortal sin.")

Heavenly Father, Your love is eternal. In Your ocean of love, You saved the world through Your only-begotten Son, Jesus Christ. Now look at Your only Son on the Cross Who is constantly bleeding for love of His people, and forgive Your world. Purify and baptize aborted children with the Precious Blood and Water from the Sacred Side of Your Son, Who hung dead on the Cross for their salvation, in the Name of the Father, and of the Son, and of the Holy Spirit. May they, through the Holy Death of Jesus Christ gain everlasting life, through His Wounds be healed, and through His Precious Blood be freed. There to rejoice with the Saints in Heaven. Amen.

Reparation Prayer for Sins Committed Against the Precious Blood
(8 February 1997)

*(My children, let me explain to you how to pray and what heaven wants from you. My Son listens to you always. He wants to hear from you always. Oh my loving children, pray this prayer **always**...at least 500 times a day."~ Our Blessed Mother)*

Most Precious Blood of Jesus Christ, save us and the whole world.

ORIGINAL PRAYER TO ST. MICHAEL
To be prayed holding Crucifix aloft
(12 January 2001)

("Raise up the Agonizing Crucifix I gave you against the power of darkness and say this prayer with the sign of the cross. Do this in the

*name of the Father, and of the Son, and of the Holy Spirit. You will conquer... **Say this prayer every day**, since the battle is great...")*

O Glorious Prince of the Heavenly Host, St. Michael the Archangel, defend us in the battle and in the terrible warfare that we are waging against the principalities and powers, against the rulers of this world of darkness, against the evil spirits. Come to the aid of man, whom Almighty God created immortal, made in his own image and likeness, and redeemed at a great price from the tyranny of Satan.

Fight this day the battle of the Lord, together with the holy angels, as already thou hast fought the leader of the proud angels, Lucifer, and his apostate host, who were powerless to resist thee, nor was there place for them any longer in heaven. That cruel, ancient serpent, who is called the devil or Satan who seduces the whole world, was cast into the abyss with his angels. Behold, this primeval enemy and slayer of men has taken courage. Transformed into an angel of light, he wonders about with all the multitude of wicked spirits, invading the earth in order to blot out the name of God and of His Christ, to seize upon, slay and cast into eternal perdition souls destined for the crown of eternal glory. This wicked dragon pours out, as a most impure flood, the venom of his malice on men of depraved mind and corrupt heart, the spirit of lying, of impiety, of blasphemy, and the pestilent breath of impurity, and of every vice and iniquity.

These most crafty enemies have filled and inebriated with gall and bitterness the Church, the spouse of the Immaculate Lamb, and have laid impious hands on her most sacred possessions. In the Holy Place itself, where the See of the most Holy Peter and the Chair of Truth has been set up as the light of the world, they have raised the throne of their abominable impiety, with the iniquitous design that when the Pastor has been struck, the sheep may be.

Arise then, O invincible Prince, bring help against the attacks of the lost spirits to the people of God, and give them the victory. They venerate thee as their protector and patron; in thee holy Church glories as her defense against the malicious power of hell; to thee has

God entrusted the souls of men to be established in heavenly beatitude. Oh, pray to the God of peace that He may put Satan under our feet, so far conquered that he may no longer be able to hold men in captivity and harm the Church. Offer our prayers in the sight of the Most High, so that they may quickly find mercy in the sight of the Lord; and vanquishing the dragon, the ancient serpent, who is the devil and Satan, do thou again make him captive in the abyss, that he may no longer seduce the nations. Amen.

L: Behold the Cross of the Lord; be scattered ye hostile powers.
R: The Lion of the tribe of Judah has conquered the root of David.
L: Let Thy mercies be upon us, O Lord.
R: As we have hoped in Thee.
L: O Lord, hear my prayer.
R: And let my cry come unto Thee.
L: Let us pray

O God, the Father of Our Lord Jesus Christ, we call upon Thy Holy Name, and as supplicants we implore Thy clemency, that by the intercession of Mary, ever Virgin, Immaculate and Our Mother, and of the glorious St. Michael the Archangel, Thou wouldst deign to help us against Satan and all the other unclean spirits, who wander about the world for the injury of the human race and the ruin of souls. Amen.

POWERFUL INVOCATION OF PROTECTION
To be prayed holding Crucifix aloft
(7 July 1997)

Adoration! Adoration!! Adoration!!! To Thee, O powerful weapon. Adoration! Adoration!! Adoration!!! To Thy Precious Blood. Merciful Agonizing Jesus Christ, pour Your Precious Blood on souls. Satisfy our thirst and defeat the enemy. Amen.

Powerful Blood of Salvation, fight the enemy. (3 times)

PRAYER FOR THE NEW ISRAEL
To Acknowledge the Value of the Price of Their Redemption
Ecclesiasticus (Sirach) 36:1-19
(20 July 2001)

Have mercy upon us, O God of all, and behold us,
And show us the light of Thy mercies:
Send Thy fear upon the nations that have not sought after Thee;
That they may know that there is no God beside Thee,
And that they may show forth Thy wonders.

Lift up Thy hand over the strange nations,
That they may see Thy power.
For as Thou hast been sanctified in us in their sight,
So Thou shalt be magnified among them in our presence,
That they may know Thee, as we also have known Thee,
That there is no God beside Thee, O Lord.

Renew Thy signs, and work new miracles.
Glorify Thy hand, and Thy right arm.
Raise up indignation, and pour out wrath.
Take away the adversary, and crush the enemy.
Hasten the time, and remember the end,
That they may declare Thy wonderful works.

Let him that escapeth be consumed by the rage of the fire;
And let them perish that oppress Thy people.
Crush the head of the princes of the enemies that say:
There is no other beside us.

Gather together all the tribes of Jacob,
That they may know that there is no God besides Thee,
And may declare Thy great works,
And Thou shalt inherit them as from the beginning.

Have mercy on Thy people,
Upon whom Thy name is invoked;
And upon Israel,

Whom Thou hast raised up to be Thy firstborn.
Have mercy on Jerusalem,
The city which Thou hast sanctified,
The city of Thy rest.

Fill Sion with Thy unspeakable words,
And Thy people with Thy glory.
Give testimony to them
That are Thy creatures from the beginning,
And raise up the prophesies
Which the former prophets spoke in Thy name.

Reward them that patiently wait for Thee,
That Thy prophets may be found faithful;
And hear the prayers of Thy servants,
According to the blessing of Aaron over Thy people,
And direct us into the way of justice,
And let all know that dwell upon the earth,
That Thou art God the beholder of all ages. Amen.

Precious Blood of Jesus Christ refine the Church and wash us clean. (3 times)

**Our Father*...Hail Mary* (3 times)...
Glory Be* (3 times)...**

PRAYER OF DIVINE PRAISE
AND ADORATION

Holy, Holy, Holy!
Blessed be the Holy Name of God.
Blessed be the Eternal Love.
Blessed be the Most Precious Blood.
All glory, honor and praise be to Jesus Crucified.
Adoration be to the Most Holy Trinity.
Amen, Amen, Amen!

ATONEMENT PRAYER WITH THE CROWN OF THORNS
As Given to Barnabas by St. Cecilia
(14 July 2000)

Chorus
(Music on page 102, 103)
I am all alone
I am all abandoned
Leaving Me with a crown of thorns,
So pierced My Heart, which pierced My Head.
All My people have deserted Me.

Verses
(1) My lovers, My lovers
Where are you, where are you?
This crown of thorns has pierced My Soul
Withdraw the thorns, have mercy on Me.

(2) For love of You, for love of You
I died on the cross with a crown of thorns.
I am living with the thorns again
I am the Agonizing Jesus Christ.

Prayer
My dearest Agonizing Jesus Christ, Son of the Most High, I fall prostrate at Your Feet with all my nothingness. I recall all my grievous offenses against You. I pray You Lord, have mercy on me. My sins kept You in agony over these thousands of years. Looking at You hanging alive on the Cross with a horrible crown of thorns, blood badly bathing Your Face, and the spikes of the thorns piercing Your delicate Sacred Face, I feel sorry for my ungrateful gift of thorns to You. I wish to withdraw the crown of thorns and offer You a loving golden crown. *(Kissing the crown and pressing it on her heart, she prayed.)*

My Jesus, Whose Sacred Head I lacerated with a crown of thorns

- have mercy on me and forgive Your world. **My Jesus, Who is suffering mystically the pain and agony of my wicked crown of thorns in Your Sacred Heart** – have mercy on me and forgive Your world. **My Jesus, Who suffers the ignominy of my wicked crown of thorns** – have mercy on me and forgive Your world.
(Pressing the thorns on her head, she kissed the Feet of the Agonizing Jesus Christ on the Cross and prayed.)

My Agonizing Jesus, I remember how I beat Your Sacred Head with an iron rod to drive the spikes of the thorns into Your delicate brain. I feel its sound and pain like a thunderbolt disfiguring Your virginal being. Oh! How callously my wickedness has pained You, my Gentle Savior. When I consider Your terrible journey to Calvary, I weep bitterly for my wicked crown of thorns on Your Sacred Head, the seat of Divine Wisdom. I feel Your falling under the Cross, with the weight of the Cross helping the spikes penetrate deeper and deeper into Your delicate brain. I saw my very self dragging You up and beating You on Your Sacred Head with a spear. Oh! Would that I was not the one who did all these things to my loving Savior. I will fight for You.

My Jesus, I have treated You cruelly, forgive me, forgive me, forgive Your world. I will do all things possible to withdraw the thorns through my own way of life henceforth. My wickedness kept the Crown of Thorns on Your Sacred Head until your death to see that You did not derive any comfort from any part of Yourself. Lord have mercy on me, Christ have mercy on my wickedness. I feel Your Sacred Head resting dead on the lap of Your Sorrowful Mother. There I saw the united hands of John the Beloved, Mary Magdalen, and Your Sorrowful Mother removing my wicked crown of thorns from Your Sacred Head with loving tears. I wish I were one of them – withdrawing my wicked crown and offering a golden crown of my love to You. *(Holding the Crown of Thorns and looking meditatively in silence, she finally prayed)*

I offer You my very self and promise to carry my cross after You all the days of my life with joy and love. Take the merits of my sufferings and persecutions, which I promise to accept with love in atonement for my sins and those of the whole world. Dearest Agonizing Jesus Christ, with this poor offering, I wish to withdraw my wicked Crown of Thorns and offer You a golden crown. Receive from me, with sincere love, this golden crown I am offering to You. Amen.

Eternal Father, I have offended You greatly for having lacerated the Sacred Head of Your only-begotten Son, the one Whom You love most. Have mercy on me. Forgive me and forgive Your world. Amen. (3 times)

THE CHAPLET OF RENEWAL
The Roses of the Glorious Reign
To be recited on ordinary Rosary beads
(7 June 2003)

Our Lady said, *"I come to offer you and the whole world another great gift from the hand of the Eternal Father. It is a gift of joy for all hearts that have received God's Kingdom, and also a gift of true repentance to all who receive it with hope. The gift is the **Roses of the Glorious Reign**...Receive it from me, for blessed are the hands that will receive it. This prayer shall be used to welcome the feast day of the Glorious Reign at Midnight from the 13th to the 14th of September, and to close the day by 11:00pm on the 14th of September before the kissing of the cross at Midnight. The prayer shall be sung and offered with candlelight adoration to welcome the Spirit of the new Pentecost. "*

Invocation of the Holy Spirit
Come, O Holy Spirit, fill the hearts of Your faithful and enkindle in them the fire of Your love. Send forth Your Spirit and they shall be created. And You shall renew the face of the earth.
L: Let us pray.
O God, Who by the light of the Holy Spirit did instruct the hearts of the faithful, grant that by the same Holy Spirit we may be truly wise and ever rejoice in His consolations, through Christ Our Lord. Amen.

Apostles Creed*(On crucifix)...
Our Father*& Hail Mary*(on first bead)...
Glory Be's* (on set of 3 beads)...

Chant
(music on page 105)
O Most Holy Trinity, Father, Son, and Holy Spirit
Hallowed be Thy Name; Thy Kingdom come
Thy will be done, on earth as it is in heaven

THE FIRST MYSTERY
The Eternal Father's Plan to redeem the world
by sending His only begotten Son
(Pause and meditate)

A voice cried out from the Highest Throne saying, "Whom shall I send, who will go and redeem the world and bring My Kingdom down to them?" In the absence of any response, Jesus the Eternal Word said, "Here I am, send Me Father."

O God, by the merit of this mystery, make me an instrument of salvation and of renewal of the world. Amen.

Our Father* & Hail Mary* (on single bead)...

L: Come Holy Spirit, come into my heart and fill the hearts of the faithful
R: And renew the face of the earth. (on 10 beads)

Glory Be*...O Most Holy Trinity*...

Chant
O Most Holy Trinity, Father, Son, and Holy Spirit
Hallowed be Thy Name; Thy Kingdom come
Thy will be done, on earth as it is in heaven

THE SECOND MYSTERY
A little girl called Mary was chosen to be
the daughter
of God the Father, Mother of God the Son
and Spouse of God the Holy Spirit
(Pause and meditate)

God sent an Angel to a little girl named Mary in the town of Nazareth in Galilee, to announce the birth of His only begotten Son. At the greeting of the Angel, the Holy Spirit descended upon her. And she conceived of the Holy Spirit. In the end, she gave birth to the Redeemer of the world.

O God, by the merit of this mystery, give me the grace of purity and of humility, so that by humility I will crush the head of Satan and by purity my soul will be Your tabernacle. Amen.

Our Father* & Hail Mary* (on single bead)…

L: Come Holy Spirit, come into my heart and fill the hearts of the faithful
R: And renew the face of the earth. (on 10 beads)

Glory Be*…O Most Holy Trinity*…

Chant
O Most Holy Trinity, Father, Son, and Holy Spirit
Hallowed be Thy Name; Thy Kingdom come
Thy will be done, on earth as it is in heaven

THE THIRD MYSTERY
God reveals His Son to the world
(Pause and meditate)

When the time came, God revealed His Son to the world. First at His Baptism in the river Jordan when God said, "This is My beloved Son in whom I am well pleased."(Mt 3:17) And again, during the Transfiguration on Mount Tabor when He added, "Listen to Him." (Mt 17:5)

O God, by the merit of this mystery, give me the grace to be what you created me to be, so as to do what you created me to do. Amen.

Our Father* & Hail Mary* (on single bead)...

L: Come Holy Spirit, come into my heart and fill the hearts of the faithful
R: And renew the face of the earth. (on 10 beads)

Glory Be*...O Most Holy Trinity*...

Chant

O Most Holy Trinity, Father, Son, and Holy Spirit
Hallowed be Thy Name; Thy Kingdom come
Thy will be done, on earth as it is in heaven

THE FOURTH MYSTERY
Jesus proclaims the Kingdom of God on earth
(Pause and meditate)

When the right time came, after fasting and being tempted by the devil, Jesus went into the cities of the world and proclaimed the Kingdom of God saying, "Repent! The Kingdom of God is at hand." He went about doing good and calling sinners back to God.

O God, by the merit of this mystery, give me the grace to proclaim Your Kingdom on earth by words and actions, so that Your Kingdom will reach the ends of the earth soon. Amen.

Our Father* & Hail Mary* (on single bead)...

L: Come Holy Spirit, come into my heart and fill the hearts of the faithful
R: And renew the face of the earth. (on 10 beads)

Glory Be*...O Most Holy Trinity*...

Chant

O Most Holy Trinity, Father, Son, and Holy Spirit
Hallowed be Thy Name; Thy Kingdom come
Thy will be done, on earth as it is in heaven

THE FIFTH MYSTERY

Triumph on the Cross

(Pause and Meditate)

'As man was defeated on the tree; man will be redeemed on the tree; so that the tree of man's downfall will be the tree of man's resurrection.' And He came to His people, but His people did not welcome Him, rather, they dragged Him to the mountain called Golgotha where they nailed Him on the Cross. On that Cross, Christ announced His Triumph saying, "It is finished." (John 19:30)

O God, by the merit of this mystery, strengthen the faith of Your little ones on earth. May they unite with Your Church to conquer the Red Dragon for the manifestation of Your Glorious Reign. Amen.

Our Father* & Hail Mary* (on single bead)...

L: Come Holy Spirit, come into my heart and fill the hearts of the faithful
R: And renew the face of the earth. (on 10 beads)

Glory Be*...O Most Holy Trinity*...

Chant

O Most Holy Trinity, Father, Son, and Holy Spirit
Hallowed be Thy Name; Thy Kingdom come
Thy will be done, on earth as it is in heaven
(3 times)

Hail Holy Queen*...

LITANY OF THE SAINTS

*In Latin, the response "**Ora** pro nobis" is made when we ask a single individual to pray for us. The response "**Orate** pro nobis" is used when we ask two or more to pray for us. All responses are printed in bold. Only respond when you see a star*.*

Latin:
Kyrie, eleison
Christe, eleison
Kyrie, eleison

Christe, audi nos
Christe, exaudi nos

Pater de coelis Deus*
*Miserere nobis
Fili Redemptor
Mundi Deus*
Spiritus sancte Deus*
Sancta Trinitas unus Deus*

Sancta Maria*
*Ora(te) pro nobis
Sancta Dei Genetrix*
Sancta Virgo virginum*
Sancte Michael*
Sancte Gabriel*
Sancte Raphael*
Omnes sancti Angeli,
Et Archangeli*
Omnes sancti beatorum
Spirituum ordines*
Sancte Ioannes Baptista*
Sancte Ioseph*
Omnes sancti Patriarchae,
Et Prophetae*
Sancte Petre*

English:
Lord, have mercy on us
Christ, have mercy on us
Lord, have mercy on us

Christ, hear us
Christ, graciously hear us

God, the Father of Heaven*
*Have mercy on us
God the Son,
Redeemer of the world*
God the Holy Spirit*
Holy Trinity, One God*

Holy Mary*
*Pray for us
Holy Mother of God*
Holy Virgin of virgins*
Saint Michael*
Saint Gabriel*
Saint Raphael*
All ye holy Angels,
And Archangels*
All ye holy orders
Of blessed spirits*
Saint John the Baptist*
Saint Joseph*
All ye holy Patriarchs,
And Prophets*
Saint Peter*

Sancte Paule*	Saint Paul*
Sancte Andrea*	Saint Andrew*
Sancte Iacobe*	Saint James*
Sancte Ioannes*	Saint John*
Sancte Thoma*	Saint Thomas*
Sancte Iacobe*	Saint James*
Sancte Philippe*	Saint Philip*
Sancte Bartholomaee*	Saint Bartholomew*
Sancte Matthaee*	Saint Matthew*
Sancte Simon*	Saint Simon*
Sancte Thaddaee*	Saint Thaddeus*
Sancte Mathia*	Saint Matthias*
Sancte Barnaba*	Saint Barnabas*
Sancte Luca*	Saint Luke*
Sancte Marce*	Saint Mark*
Omnes sancti Apostoli,	All ye holy Apostles,
Et Evangelistae*	And Evangelists*
Omnes sancti Discipuli	All ye holy Disciples
Domini*	Of Our Lord*
Omnes sancti Innocentes*	All ye holy Innocents*
Sancte Stephane*	Saint Stephen*
Sancte Laurenti*	Saint Lawrence*
Sancte Vincenti*	Saint Vincent*
Sancti Fabiane et	Saints Fabian and
Sebastiane*	Sebastian*
Sancti Ioannes et Paule*	Saints John and Paul*
Sancti Cosma et	Saints Cosmas and
Damiane*	Damian*
Sancti Gervasi et Protasi*	Saints Gervase and Protase*
Omnes sancti Martyres*	All ye holy Martyrs*
Sancte Silvester*	Saint Sylvester*
Sancte Gregori*	Saint Gregory*
Sancte Ambrosi*	Saint Ambrose*
Sancte Augustine*	Saint Augustine*
Sancte Hieronyme*	Saint Jerome*
Sancte Martine*	Saint Martin*
Sancte Nicolae*	Saint Nicholas*

Omnes sancti Pontifices	All ye holy Bishops
Et Confessores*	And Confessors*
Omnes sancti Doctores*	All ye holy Doctors*
Sancte Antoni*	Saint Anthony*
Sancte Benedicte*	Saint Benedict*
Sancte Bernarde*	Saint Bernard*
Sancte Dominice*	Saint Dominic*
Sancte Francisce*	Saint Francis*
Omnes sancti Sacerdotes	All ye holy Priests
Et Levitae*	And Levites*
Omnes sancti Monachi	All ye holy Monks
Et Eremitae*	And Hermits*
Sancta Maria Magdalena*	Saint Mary Magdalen*
Sancta Agatha*	Saint Agatha*
Sancta Lucia*	Saint Lucy*
Sancta Agnes*	Saint Agnes*
Sancta Caecilia*	Saint Cecilia*
Sancta Catharina*	Saint Catherine*
Sancta Anastasia*	Saint Anastasia*
Omnes sanctae Virgines	All ye holy Virgins
Et Viduae*	And Widows*
Omnes Sancti et	All ye holy men and
Sanctae Dei	Women, Saints of God
Intercedite pro nobis	**Interceed for us**
Propitius esto	Be merciful
Parce nos, Domine	**Spare us, O Lord**
Propitius esto	Be merciful
Exaudi nos,	**Graciously hear us,**
Domine	**O Lord**
Ab omni malo*	From all evil*
Libera nos, Domine	***O Lord, deliver us***
Ab omni peccato*	From all sin*
Ab ira tua*	From Thy wrath*

A subitanea et	From a sudden and
Improvisa morte*	Unprovided death*
Ab insidiis	From the deceits of
Diaboli*	The devil*
Ab ira, et odio, et omni	From anger, hatred,
Mala voluntate*	and all ill-will*
A spiritu	From the spirit of
Fornicationis*	Fornication*
A fulgare et	From lightning and
Tempestate*	Tempest*
A flagello	From the scourge of
Terraemotus*	Earthquake*
A peste, fame,	From plague, famine,
Et bello*	And war*
A morte perpetua*	From everlasting death*
Per mysterium sanctae	Through the mystery of
Incarnationis tuae*	Thy Holy Incarnation*
Per adventum tuum*	Through Thy coming*
Per nativitatem tuam*	Through Thy Nativity*
Per baptismum et sanctum	Through Thy Baptism
Ieiunium tuum*	And holy fasting*
Per crucem et	Through Thy Cross and
Passionem tuam*	Passion*
Per mortem et	Through Thy death and
Sepulturam tuam*	Burial*
Per sanctam	Through Thy holy
Resurrectionem tuam*	Resurrection*
Per admirabilem	Through Thine admirable
Ascensionem tuam*	Ascension*
Per adventum Spiritus	Through the coming of the
Sancti Paracliti*	Holy Spirit, the Paraclete*
In die iudicii*	In the day of Judgement*
Peccatores*	We sinners*
*Te rogamus, audi nos	***We beseech Thee, hear us**
Ut nobis parcas*	That Thou wouldst spare us*
Ut nobis indulgeas*	That Thou wouldst pardon us*

Ut ad veram paenitentiam
nos perducere digneris*
Ut Ecclesiam tuam
sanctam regere, et
conservare digneris*
Ut Domnum apostolicum,
et omnes ecclesiasticos
ordines in sancta religione
conservare digneris*
Ut inimicos sanctae
Ecclesiae humiliare
digneris*
Ut Regibus et Principibus
Christianis pacem et veram
concordiam donare digneris*
Ut cuncto populo christiano
pacem et unitatem largiri
digneris*
Ut omnes errantes ad

unitatem Ecclesiae revocare,
et infidels universos ad
evangelii lumen perducere
digneris*
Ut nosmetipsos in tuo sancto
servitio confortare, et
conservare digneris*
Ut mentes nostras ad
caelestia desideria
erigas*
Ut omnibus benefactoribus
nostris sempiterna bona
retribuas*
Ut animas nostras, fratrum,
propinquorum, et
benefactorum nostrorum
ab aeterna damnatione

That Thou wouldst bring us
to true penance*
That Thou wouldst govern
and preserve Thy
Holy Church*
That Thou wouldst preserve
our Apostolic Prelates and
all ecclesiastical orders in
the holy religion*
That Thou wouldst humble
the enemies of Thy Holy
Church*
That Thou wouldst give
peace and true concord to
Christian kings and princes*
That Thou wouldst grant
peace and unity to all
Christian people*
That Thou wouldst bring back

to the unity of the Church all
those who have strayed from
the truth, and lead to the light
of the Gospel all unbelievers*
That Thou wouldst confirm
and preserve us in Thy
holy service*
That Thou wouldst lift up
our minds to heavenly
desires*
That Thou wouldst render
eternal blessings to all
our benefactors*
That Thou wouldst deliver
our souls and those of our
brethren, relations, and
benefactors from eternal

eripias*
Ut fructus terrae dare et
conservare digneris*
Ut omnibus fidelibus
defunctis requiem aeternam
donare digneris*
Ut nos exaudire
digneris*
Jesu, Fili Dei Vivi*

damnation*
That Thou wouldst give and
preserve the fruits of the earth*
That Thou wouldst give
eternal rest to all the faithful
departed*
That Thou wouldst
graciously hear us*
Jesus, Son of the Living God*

Agnus Dei, qui tollis
peccata mundi
Parce nobis, Domine
Agnus Dei, qui tollis
peccata mundi
Exaudi nos, Domine
Agnus Dei, qui tollis
Peccata mundi
Miserere nobis

Lamb of God, Who takes away
the sins of the world
Spare us, O Lord
Lamb of God, Who takes away
the sins of the world
Graciously hear us, O Lord
Lamb of God, Who takes away
the sins of the world
Have mercy on us

Christe, audi nos
Christe, exaudi nos
Kyrie, eleison
Kyrie, eleison
Christe, eleison
Christe, eleison
Kyrie, eleison
Krie, eleison

Christ, hear us
Christ, graciously hear us
Lord, have mercy
Lord, have mercy
Christ, have mercy
Christ, have mercy
Lord, have mercy
Lord, have mercy

**Consecration Prayer to the Precious Blood
of Jesus Christ**
(page 20)

**For All Benefactors of this Devotion
Our Father*...Hail Mary*...Glory Be*...**

AN ALERT
FOR THE TWELVE TRIBES OF ISRAEL
To Exalt the Holy Cross
(15 July 2000)

(This prayer is prayed by all Apostles of the Precious Blood on September 14th, The Feast of the Triumph of the Holy Cross, which Our Lord has declared as the Feast of His Glorious Reign. On this day a devotee will lie prostrate at the specified times and adore the Lamb of God, singing each invocation when they rise. At other times, they may be prayed or sung before a Crucifix)

PRIESTS: **Oh! House of Israel**
(12 Noon)   Come! Adore the Lamb of God
                  Adore the Lamb on the Cross
                  Who died to save us all.

Chorus
(Music on page 104)
Holy, Holy, Holy!
Holy, Holy, Holy!
Holy is the Lamb
Who died on the Cross.

Verses
(1) Honor, glory and praise
Power, wealth and wisdom
Strength and might to Thee
Sacrificial Lamb
(Chorus)

(2) Thy Kingdom come
Agonizing Lord
Thy Kingdom come
Merciful Lamb
(Chorus)

(3) Reign forever Lord
Crucified Lamb of God
Who hangs bleeding for love
Reign forevermore.
(Chorus)

GROUP I: **Oh! House of Reuben** (Peter)
(1:00pm)   Come! Adore the Lamb of God
Adore the Lamb on the Cross
Who died to save us all.
Repeat Chorus with Verses

GROUP II: **Oh! House of Simeon** (Andrew)
(2:00pm)   Come!... *Repeat as above*

GROUP III: **Oh! House of Levi** (James, Son of Zebedee)
(3:00pm)   Come!... *Repeat as above*

GROUP IV: **Oh! House of Judah** (John)
(4:00pm)   Come!... *Repeat as above*

GROUP V: **Oh! House of Dan** (Philip)
(5:00pm)   Come!... *Repeat as above*

GROUP VI: **Oh! House of Naphtali** (Bartholomew)
(6:00pm)   Come!... *Repeat as above*

GROUP VII: **Oh! House of Gad** (Thomas)
(7:00pm)   Come!... *Repeat as above*

GROUP VIII: **Oh! House of Asher** (Matthew)
(8:00pm)   Come!... *Repeat as above*

GROUP IX: **Oh! House of Issachar** (James son of Alphaeus)
(9:00pm)   Come!... *Repeat as above*

GROUP X: **Oh! House of Zebulum** (Thaddaeus)
(10:00pm)   Come!... *Repeat as above*

GROUP XI: **Oh! House of Joseph** (Simon the Zealot)
(11:00pm)   Come!... *Repeat as above*

GROUP XII: **Oh! House of Benjamin** (Matthias)
(12 Midnight) Come!... *Repeat as above*

THE CROSS OF PERFECTION
(22-25 July 2000)

Sacred Scripture records:

"And therefore, we also having so great a cloud of witnesses over our head, laying aside every weight and sin which surrounds us, let us run by patience to the fight proposed to us: Looking on Jesus, the author and finisher of faith, who having joy set before Him, endured the cross despising the shame, and now sitteth on the right hand of the throne of God. For think diligently upon Him that endured such opposition from sinners against himself; that you be not wearied, fainting in your minds. For you have not yet resisted unto blood, striving against sin, and you have forgotten the consolation, which speaketh to you as unto children saying: **My son, neglect not the discipline of the Lord; neither be thou wearied whilst thou art rebuked by Him. For whom the Lord loveth, He chastiseth; and He scourgeth every son whom He receiveth.** *Persevere under discipline. God dealeth with you as with His sons; for what son is there whom the Father doth not correct? But if you be without chastisement, whereof all are made partakers, then you are bastards and not sons. Moreover, we have had fathers of our flesh for instructors, and we reverenced them: shall we not much more obey the Father of spirits, and live? And they indeed, for a few days, according to their own pleasure, instructed us: but He, for our profit, that we might receive His sanctification. Now all chastisement for the present indeed seemeth not to bring with it joy, but sorrow: but afterwards it will yield, to them that are exercised by it, the most peaceable fruit of justice. (Heb 12:1-11)*

A person's daily sufferings, borne in either patient resignation or joy, and joined to the Holy Cross of Our Lord is a mark of eternal glory. To reject sufferings, sacrifices, humiliations, and mortifications in this life is to walk the broad and easy way that leads to destruction (Matt 7:13-14). Our Lord himself clearly stated that we are to deny our desires, take up our cross daily and follow Him (Mark 8:34-36). Our Lord is calling us out of our selfish self-centered lives and into "the works (Will) of Him Who sent Me." (John 9:4).

Our Lord has given Barnabas the "Cross of Perfection," to help us do this. It is a model for carrying our own crosses. Just as there are four projections to a normal cross, there are also four graces that can be acquired by diligently applying Our Lord's teachings to the carrying of our own crosses in life. Reflect frequently on these teachings until you have collected and refined all the 'planks' and master the Cross of Perfection.

Cross of Love
(22 July 2000)

We are enjoined by Christ in the Gospel to love all His creatures on earth, even our worst enemy. *"Love your enemies, do good to them that hate you, and pray for them that persecute and calumniate you."* (Matt 5:44). One can demonstrate this love by offering Masses, prayers, and fasts for the conversion and sanctification of all those who offend, hate, or persecute us. We can demonstrate this love further by performing corporal and spiritual works of mercy on behalf of our needy brothers and sisters. This task will be dry and difficult at first, but as we persevere, this plank of the Cross will become sweet.

Jesus said: *This royal road is a gracious way for those who love Me. They see the ocean of sanctifying grace along the way. This grace is a source of power and strength for them. They embrace it and remain firm, but for those who hate My Cross, it is a stumbling road. Children, My way is easy for those who love My Cross. This way is the road of happiness since its end is a land full of happiness and joy! Mighty men have stopped on the way; they stop the moment their love for Me and the Holy Cross vanishes. Children no one can walk through this land to the land of happiness without true love for the Holy Cross. True love has no attachment to self. He has the self cru-*

cified. True love lowers itself and takes the lowest position. He chooses to serve than to be served. True love has no attachment to the world. He lays his love completely on the One who died for love of him. True love realizes that to die for the One he loves is greater than any love he will show to his Lover. True love follows his Lover wherever He goes. He rejoices with Him, and suffers with Him whenever the time comes. I am the agonizing Jesus Christ who calls you to follow Me. My way is a desert way...it is a Calvary. I am calling all My lovers to follow Me through this royal way of the Cross. I choose it for your sake. This is the way My Father has kept for Me from the beginning for your salvation. This is the way I follow to set you free, let all My lovers follow it back to our joyful home.

Cross of Forgiveness
(23 July 2000)

No person can hope to enter Heaven without total forgiveness of one's sins. Our Lord in heaven waits to hear our cries of repentance, so that He may shower our contrite hearts with the rich graces of His forgiveness. But what of those who sin against us? Our Lord himself gave us the simple rule to follow, *"And forgive us our debts, as we also forgive our debtors."* (Matt 6:12) We will be forgiven by the same measure that we forgive others. *"For the same measure that you shall mete withal, it shall be measured to you again."* (Luke 6:38) Do not wait for words or deeds of repentance from those who offend or injure you. Forgive them with all your heart the very moment you are offended. This applies even to those who would have us put to death or cause us grievous harm. Following the example of Christ, His Apostles and Martyrs of the Church, we are called to forgive our enemies everything. *"Father, forgive them, for they know not what they do."* (Luke 23:34) *"And falling to his knees (Stephen) cried in a loud voice, saying, 'Lord, lay not this sin to their charge."* (Acts 7:59) This plank is very difficult for a soul to attain, *"but with God all things are possible."* (Matt 19:26) Pray for a generous spirit of forgiveness.

Jesus said: *Forgive all who offend you and pray for all who refuse to accept your forgiveness. Forget all the pains of their injury that stamp* *your heart. Love them as your true friends. Children, even if they refuse to accept your appeal for peace, forgive them and show more love to them. Children, true love is forgiveness...I am the model of forgiveness... You are to forgive even at the cost of your life. Bless those who curse you. And have compassion on those who hunt for your life. Pray for those who persecute you. Offer more of your wealth to those who take your possessions by force...Truly I say to you, there is no grace for one who is offended if he waits for the one who offends him to ask for pardon before he forgives and forgets the injury. This is because he has received his consolation in the world. O what multiple graces for the offended one who pleads with love **to those who offend him** to forgive **him**. I say, he gains multiple graces which remit thousands of years from his Purgatory days. Children, I say to you, ask pardon of those who offend you. Do it with love. Do it with a repentant heart...I am the one whom they are persecuting. I am the one who will judge them. I am the one to pay them back. This is a royal Cross of perfection.*

Cross of Truth
(24 July 2000)

All followers of Christ must be truthful at all times. (Eph 4:14-15) Nothing false must issue from our tongues, even if we are to starve or die, especially for our faith. No falsehood was ever presented by Our Lord or Our Lady. *"..put on the new man, who according to God is created in justice and holiness of truth...put away lying, speak ye the truth every man with his neighbor.."*(Eph 4:24-25) The exalted state of spotless virginity and truthfulness are the only two marks mentioned in the Book of the Apocalypse that will be upon the 144,000 marked with the sign of God (Apoc 14:1-5).

Jesus said: *"Accept from Me the royal Cross of truth. I am the Way, the Truth, and the Life (John 14:6). All who reject the truth, reject Me. All who reject Me, miss the way. And all who miss the way, lose their lives...Those who belong to the light, hear Me and embrace the truth...If you are of the world, the father of all liars will love you, but you are the children of the truth so they will hate you...Children, you are called to speak the truth at all costs in this perilous moment of* *your days. But you shall be wise and humble. There is no excuse for you to tell lies...even at the moment of great loss...at the point of your death...even at the hour of rejection... at the result of imprisonment, I appeal to you, speak the truth...At the loss of a friendship or at the result of hardship, I appeal to you, speak the truth. I promise you, all lost shall be found...All who lie in order to gain, cancel their names in the Book of Life. They will soon see the great loss they made and will suffer the loss forever. But you at whom they laugh because you lost by speaking the truth, will gain...I will remove millions of years from your Purgatory days for any truth that comes out of your mouth. In the same way, millions of years are added to your Purgatory days for every lie that comes out of your mouth...This cross is heavy for man. For God, it is the lightest Cross. I love you all. I bless you all."*

Cross of Humility
((25 July 2000)

We are called to humble ourselves to the lowest point in imitation of Christ, His Holy Mother Mary and the Saints. Our Lord condescended to be carried for nine months in a humble virgin's womb, born in a lowly stable on a cold night, live as a refugee in a foreign land, live a hidden life as a humble carpenter, and die crucified shamefully between two thieves. In Our Lady's heart, she saw herself as nothing more than the handmaid of the Lord (Luke 1:38). In her canticle to St. Elizabeth she said, "He hath put down the mighty from their seat and hath exalted the humble."((Luke 1:52) Not proud, not self-assertive, modest in nature; this is the cornerstone of all virtues.

Jesus said: *"My children, drop the heavy Cross of pride which the evil one lifted on you and receive from Me the royal light Cross of humility...Consider that your God took the nature of man and became man. Your God abandoned His divinity and lowered Himself to the same nature as His creature...He took the lowest position. He is the poorest among the poor...so as to console those that are poor...Children, accept all humiliations with love. Quarrel not with those who falsely accuse you, rather, accept the criticism silently with love. Rejoice when they call you names...never utter a word of* *remorse...Truth will prove itself when the hour comes. I am the truth, I will not disappoint you...Even if your family may take your earthly possessions, just speak the truth and yield to the Divine Will. Even if your humility may take your personality away...submit to the Will of God...If your humility hinders your ministry or occupation...I say obey...Learn to take the lowest position among My people... You lose multiple graces by avoiding this noble work of being a servant. Who is great? The servant, or the master who receives the service of the servant? You might answer the master, but I tell you truly, the servant is great in the sight of God. Children, the little will be great and the great will be little. I appeal to all My lovers to drop the heavy Cross of pride and take from Me the lightest Cross – humility.*

THE GETHSEMANE HOUR
(20 July 1998)

"My children, I am in Gethsemane for you and all My people in the whole world. I am in Gethsemane always because of the hour that is coming, that horrible hour, so fearful and terrifying. My children, how many will survive? For the love I have for you and for all men, I am here in Gethsemane calling you to come and watch with Me. Remain in Gethsemane with Me so that you will not give up when the hour comes."

"My children, learn to make your Gethsemane Hour well. Observe it with your heart. Be brave to overcome your enemy. Teach them to the whole world and let them learn all the prayers I taught you...Learn today that this hour is blessed. Anyone who devotedly makes this Gethsemane Hour faithfully will never fall during his own hour of dryness and trials. He will be filled with power always and be courageous in these ungodly and wicked days."

Jesus has requested all His children come to Gethsemane with Him. Therefore, every Thursday evening from 11:00pm to 3:00am Friday morning is the Gethsemane Hour. The following prayers are to be offered during this time:

1. The Rosary of the Blessed Virgin Mary. (All four Mysteries, if possible)

2. The Holy Chaplet and Litany of the Precious Blood.

3. Consecration to the Precious Blood.

4. The Consolation and Adoration Prayers.

5. The Seven Anguished Appeals, the reparation prayers to Our Lord.

6. The Mystical Prayers that Our Lord offered to His Father during His Passion.

7. The Votive Mass of the Precious Blood and exposition of the Most Blessed Sacrament, where possible.

There are promises of grace made to those who observe the Gethsemane Hour. In addition, Jesus says that those who are faithful to this hour will have nothing to fear from the Antichrist.

THE GREAT MONTH OF JULY
(9 July 2001)

Jesus has also requested that we make three very important novenas in the month of July. *"To all My Apostles of this devotion who missed or will miss any of the novenas of this great month, they will not join My Apostles in any reparation for 3 years...For good reason, I can afford, but for those who forget, who are lazy, and those who care not, they shall follow My order...I say they will not receive this Rose (of Perfect Purity) or renew their consecration until the 3 years are over."*

These novena prayers can be said also at any time of the year. The same promises apply each time.

Prayers to be said for each Novena:
1. Rosary of Our Lady
2. Chaplet of the Precious Blood
3. Litany of the Precious Blood
4. Consecration to the Precious Blood
5. Consolation and Adoration Prayers
6. The Anguished Appeals
7. The Mystical Prayers

Novena of the Precious Blood
in Honor of the Nine Choirs of Angels
July 1st – 9th
(10 July 1998)

"My children, today being the last day of this Novena, receive My blessings, may my Holy Wounds heal you all. Through My pains be freed from all your burdens that held you, I renew your seal and call you sons of My Heart. May the ocean of My Precious Blood cover your families from now until a year from today. Angel Raphael, I command you to guard them. I am with you. Be blessed. This bless-

ing remains with all who fulfill this nine day Novena every year. Come with zeal to the next Novena."

**Novena of the Precious Blood
in Honor of the Holy Trinity
July 13th – 15th**
(14 July 1998)

*Our Lady said, "Adore the Precious Blood of My Son which is constantly flowing for His children in this last era; invoke it for protection always. Through the Chaplet...the kingdom of God **will come on earth**...As you have spread my Rosary, I urge you to spread this devotion. I am with you...Receive my blessing! I pray that your faith will not fail. You must struggle for life and help your brethren. I pray that you shall be one, you must love one another. I cover you with my holy Mantle in my Heart. I hide you all. I love you all. Receive this (a rose) for your sanctity and holiness. Remain in the peace from heaven."*

**Novena of the Precious Blood for Israel
July 20th – 31st**
(31 July 1998)

"My children, let My peace be with you today being the last day of this Great Novena of this year. I bless you all. Today I bathed you with My Precious Blood. Let the light of My Holy Spirit anoint your souls. All of you who zealously adored My Precious Blood in this month have been blessed with sanity of spirit and peace of heart. I will pour water on the dry land and lessen its suffering. In a wild desert, the ocean of life giving water shall flow. I will make a desert to be a forest. All who suffered with Me will reign with Me when My glory is revealed."

THE GREAT SEAL OF GOD
A Living Tabernacle in Our Hearts
(11 December 1998)

Throughout history God has used 'seals' for the marking of His chosen or remnant people. Before the Israelites of old left Egypt, they were instructed by the Lord through Moses, to splash the blood of lambs on their doorposts. This blood served as a 'seal' of protection from the Angel of death, sent to punish the Egyptians (Ex 12:21-28). A seal in the spiritual sense is the protection of a soul from the diabolical attacks of Satan and his cohorts and the strength to remain true to the faith.

Through this devotion, Our Lord's plan has been to save all of humanity from the coming Great Chastisement (Mt 24). The messages to Barnabas Nwoye make clear that man has reached the awaited hour when he must either be for God or against Him. Now heaven has granted a new message of hope and protection. The message is simple: *All devotees of the Precious Blood can receive the gift of the Seal of the Living God, as a protection against the Antichrist.* This is the same seal mentioned in the Book of Apocalypse, chapters 7 and 14.

On December 11, 1998, Barnabas saw a vision of Jesus coming down holding a chalice with a tongue of fire on the mouth of it. Divine rays flowed out of the chalice. Our Lord said, *"My children receive this; this is My Blood, the Blood of your redemption. Open your heart for My Great Seal."*

Barnabas then saw the holy chalice multiply and move into the hearts of a large number of people gathered at the feet of Jesus. Our Lord continued, *"My children, the hour that is coming soon is so fearful and terrifying. Who will survive it? This is what motivated Me to come to you and build up the tabernacle of My love. So when the hour comes, your heart will not be dry. The joy of My glory will continue flourishing inside all hearts in which I built My tabernacle of love. I will let the ocean of My Precious Blood flow constantly inside their hearts even in the greatest hour of dryness that will soon befall mankind."*

Barnabas was then allowed to understand that Our Lord was sealing His followers and by doing so, He would come down and truly live in their hearts to comfort and strengthen them in the evil days ahead. Our Lord went on to say, *My children, bring little infants to Me during these hours of Great Seal; I love them. I will save them. Listen My children, we have three great months of seal, then comes the hour…"*

Barnabas was given three special periods for when the Angels of

God would travel the earth to place the seal. The seal would be placed on devotees between the hours of Noon and 3:00pm, the hours suffered by Our Lord during His Passion.

- *Every Friday of December and the First Friday of January*

- *Every Friday of April and the First Friday of May*

- *Every Friday of the Great Month of July (The month normally devoted to the Precious Blood)*

Devotees who receive the seal will be given the strength and grace not to rush for the mark of the Beast (666) without which no one will be able to operate in the godless world (Apoc 13:16-17). These sealed devotees of the Precious Blood will resist the indoctrination of the Antichrist and will be rescued from the power of the Beast (Apoc 13:13-14), to be the remnant of God (Sophonias[Zeph]3:12-13). No evil can attack a sealed child of God, as Christ lives in it. A sealed soul enjoys the distinctive protection that God places on it for these times. This is a fulfillment of Ezekiel's vision of the protective seal of God (Ez 9:1-7).

It is worth noting that there are different types of seal. Some souls are sealed to survive the Great Tribulation with varying degrees of persecution. Some are sealed to go through it with virtually no persecution at all, especially if they have been living a rigid life of mortification. Others are sealed to die heroically for the glory of God the Father in the same manner as the great martyrs of the early Church. These manifestations of the seal will be evident during the Purification or Chastisement.

Our Lord explained to Barnabas on July 9, 1999, how heavenly hosts surround a sealed soul. *"Rejoice O Jerusalem, for in you the tabernacle of My love was built. The ocean of My Most Precious Blood will flow out and renew the world. You are surrounded by the Hosts of Heavenly Angels, who will guard you day and night. No one has the power to destroy you again."*

To receive the Seal of the Living God, a devotee must:

- Attempt to perform **five consecutive months** of Gethsemane Hours, ideally in groups of two, three or more, in a spirit of mortification. The Gethsemane Hours can be the whole observance from Thursday 11:00pm to 3:00am Friday, or at least one hour between midnight and 3:00am.

- Pray a novena nine days before receiving the seal. The novena can be made up of reciting the Chaplet of the Precious Blood for nine days or other prayers.

- Make every effort to make a retreat prior to receiving the seal.

- Make a good Confession

- Be consecrated ideally on the **third Friday of any month or periods specified in the 'seal hours' of Noon to 3:00pm, within the Votive Mass of the Precious Blood.** If however, for some urgent reason the consecration cannot take place at the specified times, then another time can be arranged. Any priest can perform this consecration. Here the devotee is presented with the Agonizing Crucifix and badge.

It is also a good practice to renew the Seal of the Living God often so as to remind the devotee of what Our Lord requires of them in this call to holiness. The renewal consists of observing the 'seal hours' given by Our Lord by remaining in a silent and prayerful attitude during these hours as much as your duties permit, attending Holy Mass and Confession along with the recital of some of the Precious Blood prayers. The Angels renew the seal everywhere, at home, at work, at school, etc. What matters is that you are aware and in a pious mood – whatever one does during these hours must be done with perfect love of God.

Our Lord said to Barnabas on July 6, 2000, *"Pray and observe the seal hour I gave you. Confess your sins to a priest with a sincere heart and repent. This is a true renewal of the seal. I will visit your souls with My Sanctifying Grace during the hour of seal. I will let My divine light chase away the darkness of your very souls. I will purify it. I will live there in fullness. When the enemy of my Holy Death comes, I will protect you. They will not destroy My temple, because the glory of your God is living there in fullness."*

Now is the time for you and all those you love to receive the Seal of the Living God as a protection against the Antichrist and the mark of the Beast!

TOTAL DEDICATION TO THE MOST PRECIOUS BLOOD OF JESUS CHRIST

The following formula of consecration given to Barnabas on April 4, 2000 to receive the Seal of the Living God, is used after the homily of the Votive Mass of the Precious Blood. Our Lord has instructed the message of April 5, 2000, be read aloud after or as part of the homily; or a simple sermon on carrying one's cross to the end will suffice.

A vision to Barnabas in the Desert of Mt. Carmel, Olo, Enugu State at 3:00pm
(April 5, 2000)

During this hour, I saw a vision of Our Lord Jesus Christ walking alone in the wilderness. Later, He came near a certain city and sat down on a rock, a few miles away from the city. He remained there and prayed for a long time. When He finished praying, He went inside the city and preached to the people the good news about the Kingdom of Heaven.

In the end, only seven people followed Him. They came out of the city and went down to the valley of the mountain not far from the city. In the valley, I saw that there were many crosses, too many to count. Jesus said to them "These are the rejected crosses which your people failed to carry. Whoever wants to follow Me, must carry his cross and follow Me. He will deny the world, deny himself, carry his cross and follow Me. The way that leads to happiness is a narrow way. It is a desert way, very dry and hard to move along. Whoever goes with Me will not walk in darkness. I will change your sorrow into happiness, your pains into joy. Those who love Me, find that My cross is light, and My way is easy to proceed. Children, whoever wants to save his own life will lose it, but whoever loses his life for Me, will find it.

The seven men replied in one voice, "We have left everything and followed you. Show us Your way and we will carry our crosses and come after You." Our Lord looked at them for a while and told them to go and inform their relatives and friends, then come back. They all left at once. Only Jesus was left. He sat down on a rock and bowed His head in silence.

Later they all returned and the journey began. Jesus began by giving them their crosses to carry. The first person complained of the heaviness of his own cross. Our Lord ordered him to choose from among the other crosses. When he began to carry them, he found that the rest of the crosses were heavier than his own. Unknowingly, he came back and picked that particular one Our Lord gave him at first and said, "Yes, this is mine." Our Lord gazed at him and calmly said, "Is it not the one I gave you?" They all took their own crosses and the journey began.

They sang and prayed as they moved along with their crosses, with Jesus in the lead. The journey was a serious one; no one cared to look back.

They passed hills and lowlands; they climbed mountains and passed through valleys. They suffered dryness in the hot desert. At one point, the faith of some of them began to fail. The journey was slow and steady, but yet some could not keep up. Some men were five miles behind Jesus, some three, others two miles. At this point, they began to suffer temptations of free will. I saw two of the men cutting off their crosses while the journey was still continuing. In the evening of the first day, they came to a great river. Our Lord Jesus Christ reached it first. He bent down and placed His own cross over the river and walked across it to the other side. The rest did the same, except the two weaker ones who had cut their crosses. They measured their crosses and found they could not cross the river. They sat down and wept and cried to Jesus, but no one dared to listen or look at them. They were left there while the others continued their journey. This happened on the first day as I saw in the vision.

The second day, they continued the journey day and night. They passed the whole day in the desert and suffered more severely than the first day. I saw that another two men thought that there would be no other river to traverse, so they cut their crosses like the first two men did.

When the evening of the second day came they were abandoned like the former ones, while the remaining three and Jesus Our Savior continued on their way. They endured the cold night, then entered the third day.

On the third day they arrived at a mountain. Our Lord stood there and pointed out to them their final destination. A land of happiness and rest! But before they could reach it, they would pass a certain city which Our Lord warned them was a sinful place. Nothing holy could be found there. He instructed them not to stop in that city and not to eat or drink anything there. The sins of that city had piled up too high towards heaven and it was awaiting God's wrath and destruction.

Our Lord said, "I am leaving you to go and look for the lost sheep of Israel. But I will be there to welcome you in the end." Immediately He vanished from their sight.

The three men found themselves alone but they took courage and moved on. Eventually they entered the city, the sinful city. They saw its glory and its pleasures. They were tempted with all the pleasures of that forbidden city. They were mocked shamefully by the people. After a time, two of them gave up and joined the people.

The remaining one, who was more greatly tempted than the others, persisted in his faith, carried his cross and entered the land of happiness and rest. Instantly, a cloud came down and covered the whole land. I saw Our Lord Jesus Christ holding a golden crown much brighter than the sun, coming down from the clouds with Angels too numerous to count. They came to welcome the only survivor.

Our Lord placed the crown on his head and made him see again, the whole journey he underwent and all the sufferings of the earth and his fallen friends. Within a few minutes he forgot the sufferings of the long journey and the heavy cross.

Instantly, the vision passed. The Holy Agonizing Face of Jesus Christ appeared and said to me, *"Son, you have seen. This is how those who follow Me end up on the way. Only a few struggle to the end. Struggle to enter the land of happiness. The way is hard, but he who endures until the end shall be saved. This vision will be made known to my Apostles on their days of consecration and renewal of their consecration. I promise to give you the Spirit of wisdom to open your heart for more understanding. The Spirit will light into the darkness of souls and renew the hearts.*

"I am the Agonizing Jesus Christ who touches you. Peace be with you. I bless you."

The Act of Consecration
(4 April 2000)

People: (kneeling) We come to the altar to offer our consecration prayer to the Most Precious Blood of Jesus Christ.
Consecration Prayer (3 times)...

(Silence)

Priest: (representing Christ) My loving children, my chosen. I am looking for you. I looked for you in the hill countries and in the low lands. I looked for you in the northern and southern regions, and could not find you. I turned to the east and west, and could not see you. I am thirsting for My lost sheep. How happy I am to see you come back! My chosen, your abandonment of Me kept Me in great agony over the past years. Where were you My lovers?

People: My Lord, my Savior, forgive me for I was lost in the world. Truly, I have sinned against Heaven and earth. I am not worthy to stand in your sight and ask pardon. If Your mercy is granted to me, may I be one of Your poor slaves? I lost my love for You, my Jesus. The power of darkness overwhelmed me. I couldn't see light but darkness. Through the darkness, the evil one showed me the pleasures and glories of this world. I was led through the evil pleasures to swim in the ocean of iniquity, and was chained in the world of the dead. I learnt there that his promise was nothing but death. I looked for help but found helplessness. In my grief under my bondage, I cried out "Who will deliver me?" How happy I was when I remembered You, my Jesus. I remembered your love for me that cost You Your life. I cried out again, "Jesus Christ save me." Your Name, 'Jesus,' broke my yoke and set me free. Here I am Lord, I come to do Your Will.

Priest: My chosen, I am longing to see you return. I have been thirsting for you for a long time. Come and embrace My love. My lovers, are you sincerely returning to Me to do My Will; never to leave again?

People: Yes, My Lord and Savior. I am sincerely back to do Your Will. I, (Name), a faithless sinner, cast myself at Your Feet to implore Your mercy. I renew and ratify today the vows of my baptism, when I promised to do Your Will. I renounce forever the man of iniquity, Satan, his pomps and works, and submit myself entirely to Your Divine Will, O my Jesus, my Savior. I am willing to follow You wherever You go. Make Your way known to me.

Priest: Now I will show you My way; My way is a narrow way, so rough and dry. Mighty men drop on this way, but it is easy for those who love Me, Jesus, Your Savior. Are you willing to follow this type of road?

People: Yes, My Lord. My Jesus I am willing. I love you. I will never forsake You again.

Priest: My way is a royal way of the cross. All who wish to follow Me will give up the whole world, then carry their crosses and follow Me. Those who try to save their own lives will lose them, but those who lose their lives because of Me and the Gospel will have them in abundance. Children, what again will deprive you of the love of Your Savior, Your God, or the love of the Cross?

People: My Lord and my Savior, nothing will deprive me of my love for You. I have left everything and followed You. My cross is on my shoulder. I am determined to follow You. My will is to do Your Will, O Merciful Jesus. Give me the grace to love You always.

Priest: Children, I have heard your manly promise to Me. I have written it in My Heart with My Blood. Listen to My instruction! **You will be tempted to reject Me, to abandon Me, to betray Me, to deny, and to crucify Me again.** But when you turn to Me to renew this consecration, ask pardon and more grace of love. I will forgive. I will pardon you, and bless you more. I say to you, DO NOT DESPAIR. (The priest places his hands upon the people and prays) Receive my blessing! Grant Your salvation to them O Lord and have mercy on these faithless sons of Yours. Look upon the blood which Your only-begotten Son shed for their salvation and forgive their sins. Cleanse the iniquities of their hearts. (+) Renew and ratify their souls. (+) Put in their hearts the seal of your salvation. (+) May their hearts be living sanctuaries for You. (+) May the kingdom of Your glory come into these hearts. (+) Father, may Your reign flow through these hearts to the ends of the earth.

People: Amen.

Priest: Father, I pray that they may love Your Son and acknowledge the value of His sacrificial death. May they stand for Him and against His enemy that is fighting His Church.

People: Amen.

Priest: Give them faith to carry Your Will which is hidden from the sight of the world.

People: Amen.

Priest: May the power of obedience and simplicity overshadow you. (

People: Amen.

Priest: May the grace of true love and true zeal fill your hearts. (+)

People: Amen.

Priest: May you all be united in the Trinitarian love with the Holy Vicar, the Pope, along with all the Angels and Saints. (+)

People: Amen.

Priest: I bless you in the name of the Father (+), and of the Son (+), and of the Holy Spirit (+).

People: Amen.

Priest: (sprinkles Holy Water on those being consecrated, then offers the badge) Receive this badge. I bless it in the name of the Father (+), and of the Son (+), and of the Holy Spirit (+).

People: Amen. (Consecration hymn is sung while the badges are pinned)

Priest: Receive this Crucifix from me. I bless it in the name of the Father (+), and of the Son (+), and of the Holy Spirit (+). May it renew your love for Me, your Savior. This is your armor. Through it you shall conquer.

People: Amen.

Priest: (Hymn and offering of the Crucifix) Remain in the peace from Heaven.

People: Amen.

(Continue with the Votive Mass of the Precious Blood. The following prayer is recommended at the end of Mass)

Solemn Blessing of the Archangel Michael
For Priests Only
(6 January 2000)

Adoration and praise to the Most Precious Blood of Jesus Christ, the source of my power. May it fill you all with strength and power. Amen.

Adoration to the Most Precious Blood of Jesus Christ which opens up the seal. May you all be sealed with the Blood. Amen.

Adoration to the Blood that opens up the ocean of Divine Mercy. May it grant you mercy in your days. Amen.

Adoration to the Precious Blood of Jesus Christ, may it reign in your hearts forever. Amen.

May Almighty God bless you, in the Name of the Father, and of the Son, and of the Holy Spirit. Amen.

THE PROMISES OF OUR LORD
TO THOSE WHO DEVOTEDLY PRAY
THE CHAPLET OF THE PRECIOUS BLOOD

1. I promise to protect any person who devoutly prays this Chaplet against evil attacks.

2. I will guard his five senses.

3. I will protect him from sudden death.

4. Twelve hours before his death, he will drink My Precious Blood and eat My Body.

5. Twenty-four hours before his death, I will show him my Five Wounds that he may feel a deep contrition for all his sins and have a perfect knowledge of them.

6. Any person who makes a novena with it will get their intentions. His prayer will be answered.

7. I will perform many wonderful miracles through it.

8. Through it, I will destroy many secret societies and set free many souls in bondage by My mercy.

9. Through it, I will save many souls from Purgatory.

10. I will teach him My way, he who honors My Precious Blood through this Chaplet.

11. I will have mercy on them who have mercy on My Precious Wounds and Blood.

12. Whoever teaches this prayer to another person will have an indulgence of four years.

THE PROMISES OF OUR LORD
TO THOSE WHO DEVOTEDLY PRAY
THE CONSOLATION AND ADORATION PRAYERS

1. My children, I promise to protect anyone who devotedly consoles and adores Me with this prayer against evil attacks. He will not die a sudden death. He will not be burnt by fire.

2. My children, I promise to protect anyone who devotedly consoles and adores Me against the attacks of evil spirits.

3. Any soldier who prays this prayer before entering a battlefield will not be defeated. No bullet will have any effect on him.

4. If this prayer is said to a woman in labor, she will have lesser pains and any woman who devotedly says these prayers will deliver safely.

5. Put this prayer on the head of any child disturbed by evil spirits, My Cherubim will protect him.

6. I promise to protect any family from lightning and thunder effects, and any house where this prayer is will be protected against storms.

7. If this prayer is said to the dying before his death, I promise that his soul will not be lost.

8. Any sinner who consoles and adores Me through this prayer will obtain conversion.

9. I promise to protect them with My Precious Blood and hide them in My Holy Wounds all who console and adore Me. Poison will have no effect on them. I will guard their five senses.

10. I promise to baptize aborted children who are killed daily in the world, and put a deep contrition on the hearts of their parents through the power of My Precious Blood.

11. All who devotedly console and adore Me with this prayer until death will join the Heavenly Armies and Choirs. I will give them the Morning Star.

THE PROMISES OF OUR LORD
TO THOSE WHO HEAR OR PRAY
THE ANGUISHED APPEALS

1. Children, whenever the Reparation Prayer is said with love, I promise to convert twelve most hardened sinners in the world.

2. I will allow my Precious Blood to flow into every soul that hears this prayer said. Their love for Me will grow.

3. I will forgive the sins of a nation that turns back to Me through this prayer.

4. They will not suffer the weight of the curses due to their sins.

THE PROMISES OF OUR LORD
ON THE CROWN OF THRONS

1. I will heal the wounds of their hearts, those who adore My Sacred Head through this Crown.

2. I will console those who console Me through this Crown.

3. I will open the ocean of the Divine Mercy on those who adore the Wounds of My Sacred Head through this Crown.

4. All who adore the Most Precious Blood from My Sacred Head through this Crown will receive the grace of Divine Wisdom.

5. I will guard their five senses.

6. When you touch this Crown with love, I will allow a drop of My Blood to fall on your head.

7. I will renew the love of a repented sinner who can mercifully adore My Sacred Head with this Crown.

8. There is always a sprinkle of My Most Precious Blood wherever this thorn is, I am not far; I am near.

9. I will crown his head with a victorious crown, anyone who adores the Sacred Wounds and Blood of My Sacred Head through this Crown.

10. I promise to show them My Sacred Head one day before they die all who love their crown and adore My Sacred Head through it, so as to have perfect knowledge of their sins and repent.

11. On 15 September 2001, Our Lady asked her Son Jesus to bless the Crown of Thorns with healing power.

THE PROMISES OF OUR LORD
TO THOSE WHO DEVOTEDLY VENERATE
THE AGONIZING CRUCIFIX

1. To prepare you for the battle, I give you My Agonizing Cruci-
    fix. I promise to protect anyone who has this Crucifix against
    the evil forces.

2. Through this Crucifix, I will deliver many from captivity.

3. Whenever you raise this Crucifix against evil power, I will
    open Heaven and let My Precious Blood flow to subdue the
    evil power.

4. I will let My Precious Blood flow from all My Sacred Wounds
    and cover all who venerate My Wounds and Blood through this
    Crucifix.

5. I promise to protect any house where this Crucifix is against
    any destructive power in the hour of darkness.

6. I promise to perform numerous miracles through this Crucifix.

7. I will break their hearts of stone and pour My love on them that
    venerate My Agonizing Crucifix.

8. I promise also to draw straying souls closer to Myself through
    this Crucifix.

9. Children, in the days of the evil one you will be able to go
    freely without any harm through this Crucifix.

Finally, Our Lord emphasized; **"Children, through this Cross I
will conquer. This Cross will soon be a victorious Cross."**

PRAYER APPENDIX

(All the prayers with abbreviations and asterisks in this book are printed here in their entirety. Memorizing these prayers is a beneficial exercise for a devotee.)

Sign of the Cross*...

In the Name of the Father, and of the Son, and of the Holy Spirit. Amen.

Apostle's Creed*...

I believe in God, the Father Almighty, Creator of Heaven and earth, and in Jesus Christ His only Son, Our Lord, Who was conceived by the Holy Spirit, born of the Virgin Mary; suffered under Pontius Pilate, was crucified, died and was buried. He descended into Hell; the third day He rose again and ascended into Heaven. He is seated at the right hand of God the Father Almighty, from thence He shall come to judge the living and the dead. I believe in the Holy Spirit, the Holy Catholic Church, the Communion of Saints, the forgiveness of sins, the resurrection of the body, and life everlasting. Amen.

Our Father*...

Our Father, who art in Heaven, hallowed be Thy Name. Thy Kingdom come, Thy Will be done, on earth as it is in Heaven. Give us this day our daily bread, and forgive us our trespasses as we forgive those who trespass against us. And lead us not into temptation, but deliver us from evil. Amen.

Hail Mary*...

Hail Mary, full of grace, the Lord is with thee. Blessed art thou among women, and blessed is the fruit of thy womb, Jesus. Holy Mary, Mother of God, pray for us sinners now and at the hour of our death. Amen.

Glory Be*...

Glory be to the Father, and to the Son, and to the Holy Spirit. As it was in the beginning, is now and ever shall be, world without end. Amen.

O My Jesus*...

O my Jesus, forgive us our sins, save us from the fires of Hell, and lead all souls to Heaven, especially those who are most in need of Thy mercy. Amen.

Hail Holy Queen*...

Hail Holy Queen, Mother of mercy, our life, our sweetness, and our hope. To thee do we cry poor banished children of Eve, to thee do we send up our sighs, mourning and weeping in this valley of tears. Turn then, most gracious advocate, thine eyes of mercy towards us, and after this our exile, show unto us the blessed fruit of thy womb, Jesus. O clement, O loving, O sweet Virgin Mary.

L: Pray for us, O Holy Mother of God

R: That we may be made worthy of the promises of Christ. Amen.

My God, My God*...

My God, my God, I believe firmly with all my heart. I hope and sincerely trust in You. Only You I will adore forever. With true repentance and love, I fall prostrate at Your Feet; I ask pardon of You for those who do not believe and do not want to believe, for those who do not adore and do not want to adore, and for those who crucified You and are crucifying You daily. Dear Jesus, I will console You all my life. Amen.

Act of Contrition*...

O my God, because You are so good, I am very sorry that I have sinned against You and by the help of Your grace, I will not sin again. Amen.

Prayer to the Most Holy Trinity*...

O Most Holy Trinity, Father, Son, and Holy Spirit. I offer You the Word made flesh, Jesus Christ, His flesh covered with Wounds and Blood, His agony in the garden, His scourging, His crowning with thorns, His rejection, His condemnation, His crucifixion and death, along with all the sufferings of Your Holy Church and the blood of martyrs, in reparation for my sins and those of the whole world. Amen.

Agonizing Prayer*...

Agonizing Jesus, I offer You my heart to be united with Your Agonizing Heart as a co-bearer of Your agony, Jesus, I wish to be in agony with You so as to hasten Your Glorious Reign of Peace. Amen.

MUSICAL SCORES

ROSARY HYMNS

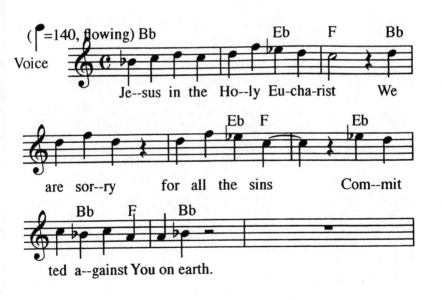

(♩=140, flowing) Bb   Eb   F   Bb

Voice

Je--sus in the Ho--ly Eu-cha-rist   We

            Eb   F   Eb

are sor--ry   for all the sins   Com--mit

   Bb   F   Bb

ted a--gainst You on earth.

CHAPLET OF THE PRECIOUS BLOOD HYMN

CONSECRATION HYMN

ANGUISHED APPEALS HYMN #1

ANGUISHED APPEALS HYMN #2

After singing the four-line stanza, go back and repeat the underline portion twice before proceeding to the next stanza.

ATONEMENT PRAYER

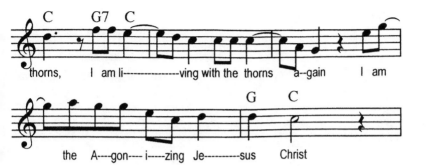

AN ALERT OF THE TWELVE TRIBES

CHANT

(♩ = 101, with deep emotion)

Voice

O Most Ho-ly Tri--ni--ty   Fa-ther, Son and Ho-ly Spir-

-it.   Hal-lowed be Thy Name.   Thy King-do-om come   Thy will be done

on Earth   as   it   i--------s   in Hea---ven

CONTACT INFORMATION

(Please send all testimonies of favors received through this devotion to the Apostolate via the Head Office's Postal Address found on page iv of this prayer book. Thank you.)

America (USA)
California
Queenship Publishing
P.O. Box 220
Goleta, CA 93116
For books and sacramentals
Toll Free: (800) 647-9882
Outside the USA: (Int'l access code) (805)-692-0043

Florida
Precious Blood Devotion
PO Box 3372
Tallahassee, FL 32315
E-mail: PreciousBloodamerica@yahoo.com

Virginia
Ms. Debra Landry
2208 Ardsmore Ave.
Chesapeake, VA 23324-1912
E-mail: my3crosses@yahoo.com

Australia and New Zealand
Mrs. Eileen Raman
3 Norfolk Crescent
Coffs Harbour 2450   AUSTRALIA
E-mail: eileenraman@mac.com

Nigeria
Lagos
(To contact Barnabas for a speaking engagement)
Mr. Fidel Aloysius-Mary Odum
Secretary General, Precious Blood Apostolate
6 Adeleke Street, off Allen Ave.
Ikeja, Lagos, 100001   NIGERIA
Telephone: (Your country code) 234-(802)-327-6517
Email: precious_blood2000@yahoo.com

Also:
Mr. Fidel Aloysius-Mary Odum
PO Box 6614
Ikeja, Lagos 100001 NIGERIA

Bank Information:
First Bank of Nigeria Plc.
Enugu, Enugu State, 400001 NIGERIA
Acct Name: Apostolate of the Precious Blood of Jesus Christ
Acct Number: 1402010113601
Note: Donations can be made by Western Union as First Bank of Nigeria
is an agent. Instruct that dollars be paid at the Nigerian end to the
Apostolate, not local currency.

Scandinavia
Ms. Annette Hoyrup
Profeti
Thursgade 20 2
DK 8900 Randers DENMARK
E-mail: anh@inter-set.dk

Singapore
Ms. Cecilia Hon
9 Greenmead Ave.
Hillcrest Park, 289402 SINGAPORE
Telephone: (Your country code) 65-(6)-466-4365
E-mail: cchon@singnet.com

United Kingdom
Kathy Kelly - Precious Blood Devotion
Padre Pio Bookshop
264 Vauxhall Bridge Road
Victoria, London SW1 U.K.
Telephone: (Your country code) 44-(207)-834-5363